D0792059

STRIPED BASS FISHING:
Salt Water Strategies

**LEARN FROM
THE EXPERTS AT**

S P O R T S M A N

MAGAZINE

CREATIVE
PUBLISHING
international

MINNETONKA, MINNESOTA

Striped Bass Fishing: Salt Water Strategies

Introduction by Barry Gibson, Editor, SALT WATER SPORTSMAN

President/CEO: David D. Murphy
Vice President/Editorial: Patricia K. Jacobsen
Vice President/Retail Sales & Marketing: Richard M. Miller

Executive Editor, Outdoor Group: Don Oster
Editorial Director: David R. Maas
Senior Editor and Project Leader: David L. Tieszen
Managing Editor: Jill Anderson
Creative Director: Brad Springer
Senior Art Director: David W. Schelitzche
Mac Designer: Joe Fahey
Photo Researcher: Angela Hartwell
Copy Editors: Barry Gibson, Shannon Zemlicka
Photographer: Chuck Nields
Studio Manager: Marcia Chambers
Director, Production Services: Kim Gerber
Production Manager: Sandy Carlin
Production Staff: Laura Hokkanen, Kay Swanson

Special thanks to: Barry Gibson, Rip Cunningham, Scott Boyan, Chris Powers,
Tom Richardson and the staff of *Salt Water Sportsman* magazine

Cover Credits: "Decisions-Striped Bass" by Mark Susinno courtesy of Wild Wings Inc.,
Lake City, MN; Gerald Almy: background surf fishing photo; back cover photos: Joel
Arrington: top left and bottom right, Dick Mermon: bottom left, Tom Schlichter: top right

Contributing Photographers: Gerald Almy, Joel Arrington, Asbury Park Fishing Club,
Bill Lindner Photography, Dick Mermon, Bob O'Shaughnessy, George Poveromo,
Tom Richardson, Al Ristori, Tom Schlichter, Doug Stamm, Sam Talarico

Contributing Illustrators: Chris Armstrong, Joseph R. Tomelleri

Printed on American Paper by: R. R. Donnelley & Sons Co.
10 9 8 7 6 5 4 3 2 1

Library of Congress Cataloging–in–Publication Data

Striped bass fishing : salt water strategies.
    p. cm.
  Articles from the experts at Saltwater sportsman magazine.
  ISBN 0-86573-113-6 (hardcover)
  1. Striped bass fishing. 2. Saltwater fishing. I. Creative Publishing international.

 SH691.S7 S74 2000
 799.1'7732- -dc21
                                     99-059350

Table of Contents

Introduction

I don't know what it is about striped bass, but I somehow caught the fever when I was very young. I first fished for them with an inexplicable focus at age seven, using a solid-glass boat rod to cast a plastic Atom plug some 30 feet into a churning Cape Cod surf. I caught nothing, but was undeterred. A few years later I actually took a few schoolies on sandworms from the same beach, then in high school purchased a well-used runabout and 30-horse outboard for $300. I caught exactly one striper from it. Another boat, a handful of bass, and then a return to the surf in a beach buggy, a Land Rover with balloon tires and a homemade rod rack. A dozen fish, tops, but I still wasn't discouraged. Next came a 34-footer and the offshore charter business, with as much bassing on the side as I could jam in. Now, 30 years later, it's back to an outboard and guiding exclusively for stripers. It's that fever that won't go away.

It can't be the fish themselves. Striped bass aren't the biggest fish in the sea, not by a long shot. They aren't the most powerful fighters when hooked, they rarely jump, and although they're handsome enough they can't match a marlin as a wall mount. When they're in a feeding mood they're

4

not particularly difficult to catch, and most people would agree that there are tastier fish on a dinner plate. Yet nearly three million anglers annually pursue striped bass along our Eastern Seaboard, and many do so with an intensity bordering on obsession.

The answer may lie in the striper's propensity to regularly confound even the most experienced of fishermen. Although striped bass are the most-studied salt water fish in America, there is much about them that we still cannot figure out, such as why they don't show up where they're "supposed to" at a given stage of the tide, why they will greedily devour a particular bait or lure one day and ignore it the next, and why a school that's feeding and thrashing on the surface will suddenly disappear into the twilight zone just as you get within casting distance. It may well be that this species' capricious behavior is coupled with just enough predictability to drive us crazy, to strike our fancy and seize our attention. We humans love a challenge, and when it comes to challenges, striped bass surely make the short list.

There are two keys, however, to a reasonable level of angling success with this species. The first is a working knowledge of the striper's habits, water temperature and food preferences, and movement and migration patterns. The second is a willingness to draw from those who have put in their time on the water and have been able to crack the code.

That's what *Striped Bass Fishing: Salt Water Strategies* is all about — giving you the benefit of experience and knowledge. The authors — Nick Karas, Al Ristori, Vin Sparano, Lou Tabory, Tim Coleman, Rip Cunningham and

Tom Richardson — are among the top striper anglers in the country, having collectively spent tens of thousands of hours studying and pursuing these magnificent fish. They are well-versed in the tackle and techniques — trolling, jigging, plugging, live-baiting and fly fishing — and know just what works (and what doesn't) in almost any given fishing situation or condition, day or night. And they're willing to share their hard-earned knowledge to help you better understand striped bass and become a more successful striper fisherman.

Just don't be surprised if you, too, catch the fever!

Barry Gibson, Editor
SALT WATER SPORTSMAN

Understanding STRIPED BASS

STRIPED BASS BASICS

Striped bass bodies are shaped much like a torpedo and fall between the extremes in fish shapes. They have a generalized fish body, the length of which is three to four times the width. The back is slightly arched, while the bottom of the body has a sway to it, especially in older fish. The tail is large and slightly forked.

Striped bass have a large, long head, almost as long as the body is deep. The pointed snout projects slightly beyond the lower jaw. The mouth is on an oblique angle, making surface feeding easier, and extends back under the eyes. Two spines on the rear of each gill cover make the head appear to extend even farther back. Large eyes are set high on the head, making it easier for the fish to see from below.

Two fins on the back are the same size and barely separated from each other. The forward fin is triangular in shape and supported by nine or ten stiff spines. The rear fin is supported by 12 to 14 rays and looks as if it had been clipped by scissors. The rays grow smaller in length from front to back. The anal fin, on the underside, just behind the anal vent, looks a lot like the reverse of the soft rear fin. The anal fin has three

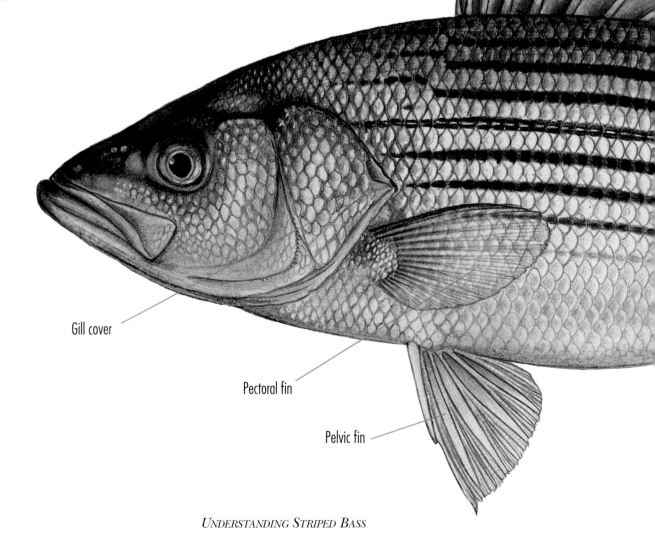

Gill cover

Pectoral fin

Pelvic fin

short spines in front, and the remainder is supported by 11 cartilaginous rays. Striped bass have paired fins just behind paired pectorals. The pectoral fins are just behind the gill covers, on a line even with the mouth.

Scales on a striped bass are large and cover the entire body, head, cheeks and gill covers. Along the lateral line, they number from 57 to 67, depending upon where the fish originate. They are ctenoid (toothed) in type and grow rings each season—helpful in determining a bass' age.

Striped bass in a marine environment are light in color, white on the bottom with a gradual darkening up the sides toward the back. The darkening occurs because seven or eight narrow, dark stripes come closer together as they approach the back. The color on the back ranges from a dark olive green to a pale blue in some fish, black in others, while the stripes or lines on the sides are black. These stripes, as well as the scales on the back, often take on a brassy reflection, while the fins and tail are somewhat dusky.

The Latin Name

The earliest scientific description of a bass labeled it as *Roccus lineatus* (Bloch). Bloch was thought to have been the first person to describe the fish in scientific journals. *Roccus* is New Latin and refers to rock, the environment around which the fish was found. *Lineatus,* also Latin, refers to the lines or stripes on the side of the fish.

Roccus lineatus wasn't a very appropriate name because it also included a Mediterranean cousin, so sometime around 1880, it was changed to *Roccus saxatilis* (Walbaum). This was accepted by most scientists until 1966 when the name was again changed. *Roccus saxatilis* is a bit redundant because it literally means rock that lives or grows around rocks, or saxatiles.

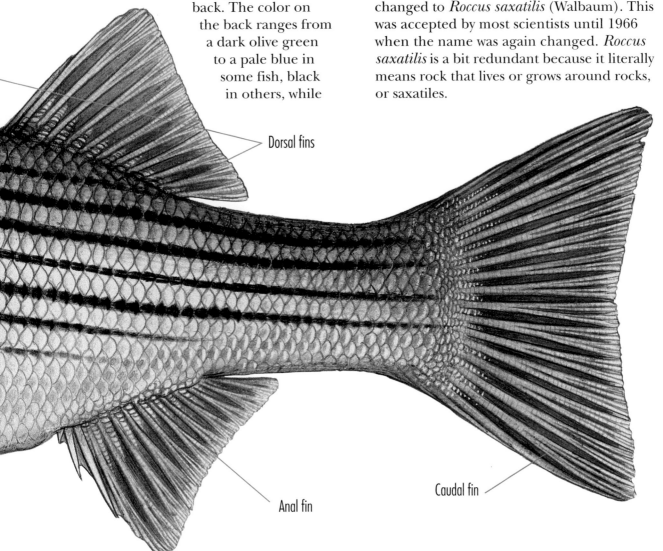

Dorsal fins

Anal fin

Caudal fin

Somewhere in the literature, taxonomists discovered that another person—we don't know his or her name—had classified the fish before Bloch. The convention is always to accept the older name, so the genus name was changed from *Roccus* to *Morone*. No one knows the exact meaning of *Morone*. It could have been the classifier's own name, since early researchers, discoverers and taxonomists commonly used their own names. Since 1966, when the renaming took place, we have had to content ourselves with *Morone saxatilis*.

In relation to other fishes, striped bass are a bony fish (some fish are made of cartilage rather than bone) and belong to the order Perciformes and family Percichthyidae. When striped bass were considered sea bass, they were included in the sea bass family, Serranidae. More recent classification has broken the Percichthyidae family into two groups, separating the warm-water sea bass of the south from those preferring slightly cooler water, like the striped bass and its near cousins the white bass and white perch.

Sizes of Striped Bass

Striped bass can and do grow to great sizes. In past years, there have been numerous records of striped bass that weighed over 100 pounds taken by commercial fishermen. There is a well-substantiated record of the largest striped bass ever hauled ashore from the waters of the Roanoke River. In April 1891, not one but several striped bass weighing 125 pounds were taken at Edenton, North Carolina. North Carolina seems to be the area for the largest striped bass, perhaps because its southerly latitude creates a longer feeding period. In a haul seine taken off the beach at Avoca, N.C., on May 6, 1876, 840 striped bass were netted that weighed a total of just over 35,000 pounds. Of these fish, 350 averaged 65 pounds each. A record from Orleans, Massachusetts, describes a striper weighing 112 pounds, and in 1887 a 100½-pound striper was taken and recorded in Casco Bay, Maine.

MEMBERS OF THE ASBURY PARK FISHING CLUB in front of John Seger's Tackle Shop during the run of big striped bass in June 1913.

Senses

Sight

Predacious fish like striped bass feed by sight. They do this very well, possibly because of their eyes. These are comparatively large, with a diameter 16 to 23 percent of the head length. The striped bass may use its hearing or sense of smell to find food, but the final approach or attack is made with its eyes. They are well placed, designed for surface feeding or feeding under an object of prey, but still able to see well ahead or below.

Striped bass eyes are a lot like human eyes. They can readily adjust to different intensities of light through changes in the size of the iris. The eyes have two types of light-sensitive cells in the retina. These cells, called rods and cones because of their shape, are used for seeing under differing intensities of light in much the same manner as the rods and cones in the human eye.

Most other fishes have cone cells that are sensitive to color and used during the day. Fish with only cone cells become inactive at night. But the striped bass is an extremely active fish that feeds throughout the night. This activity is made possible by the rod-shaped cells. The rod-shaped cells are buried behind the cone cells during the day because they are extremely sensitive to light. But as night approaches they rise to the surface and replace cone cells as the prime light and sensation gatherers.

Lenses in the eyes of striped bass are round instead of flattened, which makes the fish nearsighted. Without muscles to control the shape of the lens, fish cannot adjust their eyes and focus on far objects. Even so, striped bass get along rather well with myopic vision because most of the waters in which they swim have poor visibility. To initially find their prey, striped bass rely on the other senses. Eyes become important only when they move in for the kill.

Smell

Striped bass live in a world of smells. When an odor is waterborne, taste and smell are synonymous. Smell is the best developed of a striped bass' senses. One could almost predict that a striped bass could smell better than see just by considering the environments it inhabits. In large bays and rivers, the waters are often turbid. Once in the open, a bass doesn't go far from the beach, and in the wash there is always sand in suspension. Therefore, a striped bass is likely to smell food before it ever sees it.

Since it feeds in the dark, a striped bass needs a good sense of smell to find what it can't see. Striped bass have evolved one of the best smell/taste systems of any fish. Instead of one pair of nostrils on the head, such as many fish possess, striped bass have a double pair, two on each side. The sensation of smell is picked up by olfactory cells in the lining of the nostrils. Water that enters the nostrils doesn't go out the same entrance through which it arrived, but it does not run into the throat as it would in a human nostril. Each nostril has an exit port. This means that the fish is always tasting or smelling a fresh supply of water as it passes over the olfactory cells.

Hearing

A striped bass needs an auditory system that works in the black of night and in waters so polluted that the sense of smell is disrupted.

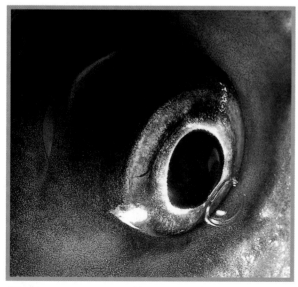

STRIPED BASS EYES can readily adjust to different intensities of light.

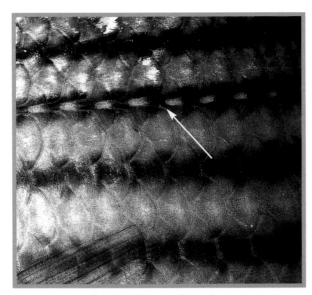

CLOSE-UP OF LATERAL LINE on striped bass (arrow).

The striped bass' auditory system can hear sounds well below our range because sound travels five times faster in the water. The auditory range of a striped bass is broad, from 15 to 10,000 cycles per second.

Fish have ears, but they don't protrude. The ears are buried in the skull, slightly behind and below the eyes. There are no external openings, but sound is transmitted to the inner ear through the flesh and bone in the skull. Sound creates sympathetic vibrations. These are carried by an electric signal to the brain and recreate sensations of food, danger, or the like.

In addition to their ears, fish have another organ that functions in much the same manner. In striped bass and most fishes, this organ is a series of canals along the lateral line (see photo above). Sensors in the canal respond to low-frequency vibrations. The lateral line is used by striped bass to pinpoint the source of a sound, like a direction finder does.

Taste

The sensation of taste is closely related to that of smell in both man and fish. Striped bass can differentiate between sweet, sour, salty and bitter tastes. The two senses do differ in range. The sensation of smell can be called the long-distance receptor, and taste, the short-distance receptor. The sensation of taste isn't a factor if you're fishing with artificial lures. But if you use live bait, the way it tastes to the fish is important, because striped bass can discriminate. If the bait is alive, taste sensations take care of themselves and won't alarm striped bass. But if you use dead, frozen, or cut bait, its condition is important. A bass will reject foods that it finds displeasing in taste. There is a diminishing order of preference: live bait first, followed by fresh-dead bait, then frozen fresh-dead bait, frozen old bait and lastly, old bait that has been in the sun without ice.

Sensitivity to Temperatures

Most fish are cold-blooded animals and have no heat-regulating mechanisms. The temperature of a fish's body is that of the ambient water. When a fish undergoes strenuous exercise, the body temperature may rise a few degrees, but the fish has no control over it. This equilibrium with the environment may be one reason why fish are so sensitive to temperature changes. A fish feels temperature through minute cells with nerve endings in the skin. These cells transmit temperatures to the brain.

The active temperature range for striped bass is wider than for most other fishes. Striped bass wintering in the St. Lawrence River have been observed feeding in water close to the freezing point. One striped bass took an artificial lure in a Connecticut river when the water temperature was 35 degrees. However, most striped bass go into a semi-dormant state once water temperature drops below 40 degrees.

On the high end, striped bass have been known to tolerate water as high as 83 degrees, although they become extremely sluggish. The optimal range for striped bass is between 55 and 68 degrees. Adult striped bass cannot tolerate temperatures above 72 degrees for a long period. However, small bass under 18 inches seem to have no ill effects in temperatures in the low 80s. A bass' preferred spawning temperature is near the middle, at 64.5 degrees. This is also the optimal feeding temperature.

—*Nick Karas*

FOOD & FEEDING

Striped bass will eat anything edible that swims, crawls or floats in its environment, even its own kind.

triped bass are voracious, carnivorous, predacious, mainly piscivorous and extremely active feeders. This may explain why, when compared to other species, striped bass are such rapid growers. They will eat anything edible that swims, crawls or floats in its environment, even its own kind. Cannibalism is not rare. The only time striped bass stop feeding is when they begin spawning, and then for only a short period thereafter.

Most foods for adult striped bass are crustaceans, other invertebrates and vertebrates. While they will eat almost everything they can find, their favorite foods include shrimp, crabs, and lobsters. They will eat all kinds of marine worms—sandworms or clamworms as well as bloodworms. Even shellfish aren't safe from bass; they will eat mussels, soft-shelled clams and periwinkles.

The kinds of finfish bass like are unlimited,

STRIPED BASS often feed together in a school. At roughly the same time, all the stripers attack a baitfish school in a feeding "blitz." The feeding ends abruptly when the bass have filled their stomachs.

but they favor menhaden, silversides, and anchovies, and at certain times of the year will feed on spot and croaker. On the West Coast, they've no qualms feeding on trout and salmon, though their favorite is the bullhead (sculpin). Other preferred fish are killifish, shad, sculpins, sand lance, mackerel, eels, squid, flounder, blackfish, tomcod, white perch, mullet, catfish, shiners and blenny. Striped bass have even been recorded eating the Portuguese man-of-war, a poisonous jellyfish. By weight, fish constitute more than 95 percent of a striped bass' diet. Though a bass may occasionally dine on lobster, the real volume comes in other fishes—most species of little or no economic value. This fish diet should be a hint to striped bass anglers who feed their potential catch a strict diet of sandworms.

Striped bass are gregarious during their younger years. Not until they become large "cows" or "bulls" do they become solitary in their feeding and schooling habits. Because striped bass feed most heavily on schooling fish, they, too, often school together when they feed. As a result, a school that feeds together usually spends its digesting time together. Thus the feeding blitz will often stop all at once, over a

rather large area of water. Another aspect of striped bass feeding habits is the great specificity in choosing a certain type of food even though many choices are available at the same time.

During the year, feeding of the greatest intensity takes place in the late spring and early summer. There is again a flurry of feeding late in the fall. Fish do little feeding during the winter. When water temperatures drop below 39 or 40 degrees, the fish not only stop feeding but go into a quiescent state, seeking out the deepest holes or warmest water in which to sulk.

Striped bass feed most actively in the evening, just after dark, then put on a second flurry just before sunrise. Successful anglers have long known that fishing is far more productive after dark than during the day. This doesn't imply that striped bass don't feed during the day. It does mean that striped bass will feed better and more consistently between sunset and sunrise.

Tides, Currents and Striped Bass

Water flow affects where, when and how striped bass will feed. Most currents in bays and estuaries, and along the barrier beaches

CURRENT, whether it is caused by tidal or riverine forces, directly affects where the striped bass and its prey position themselves within a particular water column. Stripers try to position themselves in an area where they expend as little energy as possible while gaining the most energy from captured prey.

on the coast, are caused by the rise and fall of the tide. However, in some areas, riverine currents also contribute to making water move, especially above the high tide mark. Current determines the orientation, or position, of both food and predator fishes in the water column. Fish at rest or waiting for prey to come their way always face upcurrent because it is on the current that the scent of food is carried. The ever energy-conscious fish wait at rest for it to come their way.

Some anglers prefer to fish the flood and others the ebb tide, claiming one is more productive than the other. Fish, however, feed on both tides and select the best location with respect to the current's direction. The real reason one tide may be more productive than another is based on the physical characteristics of where you are fishing. Fish may find it easier to set up behind boulders or rock outcroppings when the current flows in one direction and not the opposite. One may afford the fish a leeward respite while the other demands they expand energy to stay in the location. What the angler must do is determine, though trial and error, which places produce better on which tide and not be duped into thinking

that one is always better than the other.

Most anglers will move on the turn of the tide. In some places, this occurs almost instantaneously. In other locales, it may take an hour or more for the current to make up. Generally, fishing on the turn of the tide is poor because baitfish scatter and bass are en route to a new feeding station. However, there are places in the bass world where fishing is best on slack water.

There is one area that produces better on the flood than the ebb. It is along a shoreline. In this case, fish move in with the flood seeking new areas opened by the expanding water. This is also true in riverine locations when the tide moves upriver, overpowering the stream's natural flow. The opposite scenario is true on an ebbing or falling tide. In this instance, fish may vacate an area well before it is dry to avoid being stranded.

In the last analysis, understanding which currents and what tide are the best producers is up to the angler. It will require some field work unless you can depend upon other anglers who have already worked out the fish's preference. However, don't rely totally on what the other guys say.

—*Nick Karas*

HABITAT & DISTRIBUTION

Striped bass are basically littoral (living near shore) in their choice of marine environment, though they are capable of swimming anywhere they desire. The bass' life is closely associated with the shore front—estuaries, bays and tidal rivers—and seldom does it stray far offshore. In their early evolutionary history, striped bass were riverine fish, but they eventually learned to go down to the sea and feed in estuaries. The primary motivation for this characteristic was either species crowding or a search for food, probably both. The secondary, more recent motivation in southward-flowing rivers and along the coast was the need to escape advancing glaciers. Because they are anadromous, the fresh water populations could escape glaciers by the sea route. Today, 20,000 years after the retreat of the last glacier, the estuaries and large bays near river mouths are still the bass' prime living space.

Striped bass, during the earliest colonial times, were found in almost every stream that entered the ocean, from the St. Lawrence River south to Florida, and from western Florida to Texas. Every river had its own distinct spawning population of bass that spent summers at the mouth of the rivers or along outside beaches, not far from the ancestral stream. With the advent of winter, smaller fish migrated upstream or joined larger fish to winter-over in large, deep-water holes in the estuary. Some large fish, however, migrated southward along the Atlantic coast in late fall. Small groups of this southward migration would often break away from the main body and winter-over in a semi-dormant state in deep holes in numerous back bays and deep tidal rivers along the coast, usually behind barrier beaches from Rhode Island southward to New Jersey. Chesapeake Bay stocks would

winter-over in deep holes at the southern end of the bay or move offshore, in 40 to 60 feet of water, along the Virginia-North Carolina coasts. Then came man.

As industrialization spread over New England during the middle of the 19th century, the demand for power to turn the wheels of progress increased and eventually even the largest rivers of the Northeast were dammed.

In effect, the dams stopped all striped bass in this region from reaching the fresh water necessary in which to spawn. Within a 40-year period, striped bass production, and eventually the fish populations that had spawned here, were eliminated from this part of their range. The only major river that was not dammed was the Hudson River, the country's second largest striped bass nursery.

Maine

Striped bass in Maine are virtually all seasonal migrants with only some slight winter holdover. At one time, striped bass spawned in many Maine rivers, but barrier dams largely eliminated these sites. Recently, they have returned to cleaned rivers. Where dams haven't been removed, fish ladders were built for stocked salmon. Striped bass have no difficulty, to the chagrin of salmon-only fisheries managers, in ascending fish ladders. Some spawning has been recurring, but only in minimal proportions.

The number of striped bass in Maine's coastal waters varies from season to season, dependent upon water temperature, the appearance of baitfish that striped bass feed upon and follow, and the size of the coastal migratory stock. Consistently, when fish do appear, the Saco and the Kennebec are two of the best rivers. Generally the bulk of the fish appear from Kittery on the New Hampshire border to Penobscot Bay.

New Hampshire

In all of New England, striped bass nowadays are seasonal migrants except for occasional holdover fish that become somewhat dormant and contribute only slightly to the fishery. In New Hampshire, the distribution of the fish includes the bays and this state's short coastline. The Piscataqua River also holds good numbers of migrants during the summer months.

Massachusetts

From late April through October, bass are distributed from the estuary formed by the Merrimac River and Plum Island south to the waters surrounding Cape Ann, Boston Harbor and on down to Cape Cod Bay, and in all the bays, inlets and estuaries along the seaward and southern sides of the cape's hook. During the summer, striped bass are well dispersed about Nantucket, Martha's Vineyard, the Elizabeth Islands and the numerous bays of Buzzards Bay, as well as in the Cape Cod Canal.

Rhode Island

Rhode Island has good striped bass distribution in the waters of Narragansett Bay as well as outside the bay, along the beaches from Sakonnet Point to Watch Hill. At times of low numbers of Chesapeake migratory stocks, the western edge of Rhode Island, near Watch Hill, appears to be the western limit for summering populations. However, Hudson River stocks have continually moved eastward in increasing numbers.

Connecticut

Connecticut's waters receive striped bass from two sources. The Atlantic coastal migratory stock expands in late spring and early summer into the state's eastern waters, in Long Island Sound, when Chesapeake stocks are high. Along the western coast of the state, striped bass are more likely to be summering stock from the Hudson River fishery. From Bridgeport to Old Lyme, there is an overlap in the composition of fish from both the Hudson and Chesapeake Bay. This line is not fixed and has moved eastward in recent years. Striped bass fishing activities are concentrated at the mouths of the Connecticut and Thames Rivers, at Bartletts and Hatchett Reefs, among the offshore islands in western Long Island Sound, and at the mouth of the Housatonic River.

New York

Like Connecticut's fishery, New York's striped bass populations are composed of two different stocks of fish. Atlantic migratory stock appears on the south shore of Long Island from April to November and even as late as December. These fish are on the move, though portions do stay the summer near Montauk Point, in Gardiners Bay, in the Peconics and in Long Island Sound east of Wading River. Part of this migratory stock becomes resident in waters around Plum Island, Great and Little Gull islands, in the Race and around Fishers Island.

The largest resident stock of striped bass in New York waters are produced in the Hudson River and dominate populations in western

Long Island Sound. Striped bass inhabit the Hudson as far north as Poughkeepsie, with some fish present in the river as far north as Albany during the summer. Nursery stock, for the first two years of life, remains in the area around Stony Point before taking part in a local seasonal migration.

Adult striped bass in the Hudson are migratory, but only in a local sense. About mid-April, adult bass and those that have spawned begin a southward migration out of the Hudson. They eventually establish a summer population with its greatest concentration in New York's Upper Bay and Lower Bay and in the bays and estuaries of northern New Jersey. Those fish that enter the Atlantic move east along the south shore of Long Island and summer from Jamaica Bay east to Moriches and Shinnecock Bays.

Another portion of this fishery migrates out of the Hudson through the East River and into Long Island Sound. It spreads across the coast of Westchester County and as far east along the Connecticut shore as New Haven. The fish also spread along the north shore of Long Island as far as Port Jefferson. In times of high abundance, they move as far east as Fishers Island Sound.

New Jersey

The bulk of New Jersey's coastal fishery is composed of the migrant Chesapeake Bay stock. In the spring, as they head northward, they spread along the beaches from Cape May to Sandy Hook, and again in this same area as they return south in the fall. A second contribution of migratory stock that in recent years has increased both in its size and the role it plays here comes from the Hudson River. These fish are spread in New Jersey in waters from Newark Bay south to Barnegat Bay. They are summer residents in Raritan Bay and Navesink and Shrewsbury Rivers. During their northward migration, some Chesapeake Bay fish will spread in the large bays of New Jersey and concentrate there for a while. During the fall migration southward, many large bass do not elect to return to more southerly waters, and wintering populations have been observed at Great Egg Harbor and the Mullica River on Great Bay.

Delaware

Delaware's fish are concentrated in Delaware Bay, along both Delaware and New Jersey shores, and about the estuaries near Woodland Beach. In recent years, as the Delaware River has been cleaned of industrial and municipal pollution, striped bass have been found farther north in the river. The Chesapeake and Delaware Canal, near the head of the bay, has become a major migratory shortcut for itinerant bass moving out of Chesapeake Bay. At times, they are abundant in the canal. Studies show that the canal acts as a breeding area for striped bass, and the waterway has developed an annual spawning population. There is limited spawning in the Delaware River just below Philadelphia.

Chesapeake Bay

Shared by Maryland and Virginia, this vast body of water is the major nursery for the Atlantic's migratory striped bass. They are spread throughout smaller bays and rivers at various times. Coastal portions of Maryland and Virginia receive fish only during migrations, and there's little surf fishing except in these periods. The bay shouldn't be considered as one entity when dealing with management of striped bass because individual stocks from all its rivers show great diversity in their biology, distribution and migration.

Based on their origin, striped bass populations in Chesapeake Bay can be divided into three groups. There's an upper bay group of striped bass that is spawned in the Susquehanna River, the upper bay itself, the Chesapeake & Delaware Canal and the Northeast, Elk, Bohemia and Sassafras Rivers. The second, the eastern shore group, is composed of rivers with the same unique physical characteristics. They drain the low-relief Delmarva Peninsula and include three relatively large rivers, the Chester, Choptank and Nanticoke, and three lesser tidal rivers, the Wicomico, Manokin and Pocomoke. The third, the lower bay group, all on the Western Shore, consists of Patuxent River in Maryland, Potomac River in Maryland and Virginia, and the Rappahannock, York and James Rivers of Virginia. The lowest river in the bay is the James River; its fish are the least migratory of the bass produced in Chesapeake Bay. They more closely resemble striped bass of Albemarle Sound (North Carolina) in migration characteristics as well as racial features.

North Carolina

During winter months, there's a large concentration of striped bass located offshore in the Atlantic that does, from time to time, approach beaches from Cape Fear to Virginia Beach. North Carolina's striped bass sources are divided into two distinct groups. One is composed of fish produced in the Tar and Neuse Rivers and associated small tributary streams that empty into Pamlico Sound; the other is composed of fish produced in the Roanoke River and its associated tributaries that flow into Albemarle Sound. This latter fish stock is the largest in North Carolina and also differs from other North Carolina stocks in that it occasionally does make minor contributions to the Atlantic migratory coastal population, even though it differs substantially from more northerly stocks. In more recent years, however, it has proven to be more similar, with non-migratory tendencies, to Pamlico Sound stock.

South Carolina

From Cape Fear, North Carolina, south to Florida and along the Gulf of Mexico, striped bass are more or less confined, of their own volition, to fresh water river systems during most of the year. Only occasionally are they found in the estuaries. The farther south one travels the more this characteristic is an intrinsic part of the fish's habits. In some systems, stripers are found 150 to 200 miles from salt water.

Estuarine environments conducive to holding striped bass are plentiful in South Carolina. However, bass this far south in their distribution spend more time in fresh water rivers than in estuaries. Each river system in the state has self-sustaining populations. From north to south, striped bass are distributed in the Waccamaw and Pee Dee Rivers, which share a common estuary, and the Santee, Cooper, Wando, Ashley, Edisto, Ashepoo and

Combahee Rivers. South Carolina shares with Georgia the Savannah River, a system which historically supported a fairly consistent striped bass fishery.

Georgia

At one time Georgia had an extensive fishery for striped bass. A fair fishery occurred on the Savannah and Ogeechee Rivers. Migration runs on the Savannah took fish more than 180 miles upriver. Over the years, these rivers became polluted by pulp operations, and the Corps of Engineers' development of Savannah Harbor caused salt water to reach traditional spawning grounds. Spawning sites were so reduced that by 1980 the striped bass population collapsed. It wasn't until 1987 that a restoration effort was begun.

In 1974, a striped bass hatchery to enhance the coastal fishery was established at Richmond Hill. But because of the drastically altered marine environment, hatchery stock was used instead to establish striped bass populations in impoundments throughout the state. Corps of Engineers projects on the Savannah that contaminated the back rivers with salt water were eventually removed, and the fishery has been making a comeback. Recreational fishing on the river was halted in 1989 to help restore the stocks at a faster pace, and natural reproduction has recurred.

Although Georgia has no Gulf Coast striped bass fishery because it is blocked from the Gulf by the Florida panhandle, it does have stocks of Gulf of Mexico striped bass—glacial anomalies that are still active today in several rivers that originate in Georgia and flow south through Florida to the Gulf of Mexico. Georgia has worked closely with Florida to continue, protect and enhance this fishery.

Florida

To the surprise of most northern anglers, Florida possesses a unique striped bass fishery. The distribution is in two separate populations. One is composed of fish that make up the most southerly limit of the Atlantic Coast population. The second is composed of a Gulf Coast population that, because of a temperature block, cannot round the Florida Keys and has no contact with Atlantic fish.

On the Atlantic Coast, distribution is limited to three rivers that empty into the ocean in the northeast corner of the state. St. Marys River, a border river shared with Georgia, contains some striped bass. Within the city limits of Jacksonville, and just south of the St. Marys, is Nassau River, and in Jacksonville proper, there's the St. Johns River, both with striped bass populations. The St. Johns flows north from Washington Lake for about 200 miles before it reaches Jacksonville. Striped bass have been taken along its entire course. Striped bass have been taken along the Atlantic beach as far south as Fort Pierce, but biologists consider these stragglers or wandering fish.

Gulf Coast Distribution

At the turn of the century, the Gulf Coast states—Texas, Louisiana, Mississippi, Alabama and Florida—had substantial striped bass fisheries, both recreational and commercial. However, these riverine populations suffered a setback when their headwater environments were altered by the construction of dams for flood control, channelization for navigation and hydro-electric power for rural electrification. This, coupled with uncontrolled farm use of insecticides and pesticides after World War II, further reduced remnant Gulf Coast populations. By 1960, coastal populations had been eliminated from almost all these south-flowing rivers except for a few in northwestern Florida. The only known indigenous population of original stock along the Gulf Coast today exists in the Apalachicola-Chattahoochee-Flint river system.

The Gulf States Marine Fisheries Commission, in 1967, with limited federal funds from the Anadromous Fish Conservation Act, received money for research and management of striped bass. Its primary goal was the reestablishment of a coastal population. But first, it had to enhance the environment. All five states began habitat studies that included water quality and ecological evaluations. These led to the enactment of conservation, management and pollution abatement measures that would create a favorable environment for striped bass restoration. By 1986 some 84 million fry and fingerlings were stocked in the Gulf's coastal waters. Within just a few years, striped bass again appeared in recreational catches.

Florida

On the west coast, striped bass appear in all the rivers from the Suwannee west to the Perdido. These include the Aucilla, St. Marks, Ochlockonee, Apalachicola, Chipola, Choctawhatchee and Yellow Rivers. The Apalachicola is the most productive by far, and 40-pound striped bass are not uncommon. The Apalachicola splits into the Flint and Chattahoochee rivers where it enters Georgia.

Before 1976, when Florida began stocking striped bass in the Apalachicola River, the annual spring survey in the river's tailwater below Jim Woodruff Dam always numbered less than 200 fish. Supplemental stocking began in 1980, and the 1990 survey revealed a record 1,140 fish. Striped bass spawning has been documented in the Flint River in Georgia, the Apalachicola, the lower Ochlocknee River, which drains Lake Talquin, and the Choctawhatchee River in Florida's western panhandle.

In 1967, Florida's Game and Fresh Water Fish Commission began a striped bass restoration effort by attempting to culture and stock a limited number of native St. Johns (east coast) and Apalachicola river fish in fresh water. Since 1976, Lake Talquin has annually produced sufficient Atlantic striped bass brood stock to meet the demands for hybrid and striped bass production in Florida. Attempts to reestablish striped bass populations using Atlantic strains in several Gulf Coast rivers, such as the Ochlockonee and Choctawhatchee, have had only limited success.

Alabama

The longest migration route taken by striped bass in fresh water in the U. S. occurs in two Alabama watersheds. Both the Tombigbee and the Alabama Rivers flow into a common estuary in Mobile Bay. North of Montgomery, the Alabama divides into the Coosa and Tallapoosa Rivers. Alabama's record striper, a 55-pounder, was taken on the Tallapoosa. Striped bass are distributed along the entire route of this watershed. They are rare in the estuarine portion, though in past years they were taken there by commercial fishermen.

Mississippi

Seven rivers in Mississippi have varying concentrations of striped bass. They are the Pascagoula, Tchouticabouffa, Biloxi, Wolf and Jordan. Mississippi shares with Louisiana two rivers with striped bass, the Pearl and Tangipahoa. There was no recent marine fishery for striped bass until 1969 when Mississippi inaugurated its Gulf Coast striped bass restoration program. By 1980, an active recreational sport fishery had developed, and striped bass now are one of the major species popular in marine fishing contests along the coast.

Louisiana

In recent times, striped bass occurrence in Louisiana has been sporadic. Habitat recovery in Louisiana was slower than elsewhere and hindered reestablishing coastal populations. Louisiana's Department of Wildlife and Fisheries began its program in 1964. From 1965 to the mid 1970s, the Department received Atlantic strain striped bass fry from South Carolina and stocked them in impoundments and coastal streams. By 1976, Toledo Bend Reservoir had developed enough brood stock to support a Louisiana hatchery program. From 1967 to 1989, Louisiana stocked over 3.5 million fingerlings and 2 million fry in its coastal waters. Coastal anglers are now taking fish from the Atchafalaya, Mississippi, Sabine and Pearl rivers as well as their estuaries. They range in size from 12 to 20 pounds, but commercial fishermen have taken striped bass over 25 pounds in hoop nets. Haul seine nettings by biologists in these rivers have produced large numbers of fingerling striped bass and show that natural reproduction is occurring.

Texas

In light of their recent status, it seems almost impossible to comprehend that in 1890, striped bass were the foremost fish species taken commercially by the bay-seine fishery in the coastal bays of Galveston, Corpus Christi and Aransas. The last commercial landings from these bays were recorded in the mid-1940s, with only occasional recreational catches occurring since then. In the late 1960s, planners in the Texas Parks and Wildlife Department realized that demands for better recreational fishing were growing and the restoration of striped bass to the coast could solve that problem. They set out to produce an adult striped bass population throughout the original range of the fish along the Texas coast.

Sampling efforts on the Trinity River produced striped bass eggs and larvae, verifying that natural production is again occurring. And nighttime sampling produced juvenile striped bass. However, an adequate natural recruitment into the fishery today is still a problem, and to maintain the sport fishery at its present level requires an active stocking program. To meet this need, the department expanded its hatchery capabilities at Possum Kingdom, Dundee and San Marcos Hatcheries.

Introduction to the West Coast

The entire striped bass fishery on the Pacific coast had as its origin 132 striped bass from the Hudson River stock that were netted in July 1879 in the Navesink estuary in New Jersey, and a second stocking of 300 bass three years later from the Shrewsbury River, also Hudson River stock. Most of the stock was composed of fish between 1.5 and 3 inches. A few years ago, an estimate of the striped bass population in the San Francisco Bay complex placed the population at three-quarters to one million fish 16 inches or longer. It had been as high as three million, but striped bass in the San Francisco Bay area have fallen on hard times.

Today, striped bass are plentiful along the Pacific coast in the San Francisco Bay area and the Coos Bay-Umpqua River region in Oregon. They are sporadic on the Columbia River system between Oregon and Washington and have been caught as far north as Alberni Inlet in Barkley Sound in British Columbia. Bass have appeared in northern Mexico and southern California, but not with any degree of dependency.

Ten years after their planting in San Francisco Bay, striped bass were so well established that further stocking wasn't needed. Attempts at other West Coast locations were tried, but these failed. Conditions elsewhere that would support striped bass reproduction didn't exist. Instead of heading south, striped bass exhibited their temperate water penchant and headed north from San Francisco Bay. On their own, these vanguard fish moved into Coos Bay in Oregon. The bay was to their liking because it contained all the elements necessary to create a self-sustaining population. The fish thrived so well that by 1922 a commercial fishery was underway. Eventually, striped bass reached as far as the Columbia River, and there, too, established a breeding population. However, these fish eventually disappeared.

—Nick Karas

MIGRATIONS OF STRIPED BASS

Migration of fish is a natural phenomenon and all fishes, sometime in their lives, move about from place to place. Several reasons motivate them to move and can be divided into seasonal, spawning, and coastal migrations. By far the most spectacular are spawning migrations, as exemplified by the Atlantic salmon or the American eel. Few fish spawn where they live and eat, even fish whose entire lives are contained in one river.

Spawning Migrations

Striped bass are endowed with an instinct similar to salmon and return to spawn in their native fresh water rivers. While the specificity of salmon is uncannily exact, striped bass need only to return to the general area where they were spawned to satisfy the same urge. Actual spawning areas of striped bass are far more limited than those of salmon. To compensate for this, striped bass larvae and fry can immediately move into a light saline or brackish environment to grow.

In fall, striped bass move from one place to another in a seasonal migration. A portion of the population prefers to winter in fresh or nearly fresh water, often not far from future spawning sites. Others, however, winter in the open ocean and make long pre-spawning migrations to these sites. After spawning, the fish will migrate downriver and spend most of the summer in estuaries or along the immediate beaches, only to return again in late winter to await another cycle.

Spawning migrations are normally composed of adult fish. A striped bass is considered adult when it is capable of spawning. In males, this occurs when they are two or three years old. In females, it is much later. In rivers south of Cape Hatteras, spawning first occurs in precocious females at three years of age, but in the majority, females are four or five years old. By nine years of age, all female bass are capable of spawning. Females in certain rivers in Chesapeake Bay don't usually leave their nursery areas until the beginning of their third year. They join older migrants that have wintered offshore and are returning to spawning or summer feeding grounds.

Spawning migrations are of several varieties. Bass that live most of their lives in salt water or estuarine environments move from salt to fresh when their time to spawn is near. In river systems that are totally fresh water, striped bass will move from wintering in lower, deeper sections to upper areas with more moving water to spawn. Some actually seek rapids in which to spawn. In some river systems the migration is over tremendous distances. One of the longest spawning migrations in the eastern United States is performed by striped bass in North Carolina.

Wintering fish move from offshore waters on the Outer Banks, inshore over Albemarle Sound, and then up the Roanoke River to Roanoke Rapids, more than 180 miles upstream.

In Chesapeake Bay, basically a brackish body of water, most spawning fish winter in deeper parts of the bay or with a large contingent of older fish mixed with other itinerant bass off Cape Hatteras. Those fish that stay in the bay take part in a southern migration to lower and deeper parts of the bay as winter nears. As April and May approach, they begin heading for various rivers throughout the bay to spawn.

In colonial times on the Delaware River, spawning occurred from Philadelphia as far upstream as Port Jervis in New York. But as the valley became industrialized, pollution made these journeys impossible. Only fish capable of spawning at the river's head-of-tide water, where the salinity is zero or nearly so, were able to continue their strains. Today, confirmed spawning is again taking place in the river near Philadelphia. As pollution cleared, some bass moved as far north as the east and west branches of the river in New York.

The Hudson is essentially fresh water, or brackish in its lower sections, and spawning in various degrees occurs from Dobbs Ferry just south of the Tappan Zee Bridge north to the base of the Troy Dam. However, two major areas have been identified. The most intensive spawning taking place from Bear Mountain north to Cruger Island, with its center near West Point. A second intensive site has been discovered farther north in the Hudson, between the towns of Kingston and Catskill.

Coastal Migrations

The typical striped bass makes only two types of migrations—spring spawning migrations and winter-summer feeding migrations to grounds in the estuaries or lower portions of their river system. Post-spawning migrations are usually to lower parts of the bays or to estuaries with the intent of feeding throughout the summer. Some migrations are temperature-oriented movements so fish can stay in water best suited to their metabolism. These may be short in distance and duration and take place in the heat of late July and early August. These migrations are more typical of Gulf Coast populations.

One strain of striped bass in the Atlantic is atypical of the expected striped bass model. This group undertakes the longest migrations possible for striped bass. It's so spectacular in numbers of fish that it overshadows other non-migrant coastal bass populations encountered en route. For a long time, this migration had confused the true picture of the typical striped bass life cycle and migration patterns.

These fish stem from Chesapeake Bay stock. There are three, possibly four, definable populations of striped bass in Chesapeake Bay. One is those fish produced in the lower bay, in the James River; another is from the York and Rappahannock Rivers. These join with Potomac River fish. The third group is composed of bass from rivers in the upper bay, the bay itself, and the Eastern Shore. Not all the different stock from these different rivers contribute every year to this coastal migration. Some never do.

For some not yet totally explained reason, striped bass indigenous to the middle bay rivers—principally the Potomac River, and at other times from the upper bay—in the early 1920s suddenly and uncharacteristically undertook a vast post-spawning coastal migration north in spring. The motivation for this migration has never been fully established. Some biologists speculate that during dominant year-classes, the bay is overcrowded and food scarce. Only juveniles stay in the bay throughout summer. These fish, primarily females, typically spend their lives there until they reach two years of age and are beginning their third year. Then they feel a sudden urge to leave the bay. This is not a spawning run; most of the females are sexually immature. In their exodus, they use the Chesapeake and Delaware Canal at the northern end of Chesapeake Bay and migrate up the Atlantic coast.

There is no historical evidence of this great coastal migration until the early 1920s. It occurred, coincidentally, with the enlargement by the U.S. Corps of Engineers of the Chesapeake and Delaware Canal. When the canal was first opened in 1829 it handled only small barge traffic. The 1921 enlargement allowed much larger vessels to transit the canal between the two bays, and a much greater water exchange.

While en route, often at a point near Cape May, New Jersey, the smaller bass are joined by much larger and older fish. Some are Chesapeake bass on a post-spawning migration; others are mature fish that have wintered offshore in North Carolina or have stayed in deeper bays and estuaries along the coast. These are on a pre-spawning migration to their northern natal streams. The migration begins in late March. Non-spawning fish continue past New Jersey, eastward along the coast to Long Island, past Montauk Point and on to Cape Cod. During some years, they go as far north as the Gulf of Maine and summer in the Canadian Maritimes.

As this group passes north of Long Island it begins to fragment. Some drop off along the way to summer in bays of eastern Long Island, Connecticut, Rhode Island, off the Elizabeth Islands, and on both sides of Cape Cod. Even a few fish produced in North Carolina waters take part in the migration, but researchers have shown their contribution to be minimal. North Carolina fish, along with those of the James River in Chesapeake Bay, instead summer in Albemarle and Pamlico Sounds or the lower Chesapeake Bay.

The migratory habits of striped bass from the Hudson River nursery exhibit the more typical migrations characteristic of other striped bass populations. Fish produced in the Hudson make a relatively short southward migration, spending summers in lower New York Bay, tidal rivers in adjacent New Jersey, and eastward along the Atlantic as far as Jamaica Bay and western Great South Bay.

In Long Island Sound, Hudson River stock summer along the Connecticut shore as far east as Bridgeport and on Long Island's north shore about as far east as Port Jefferson and Mt. Sinai Harbor. Though this is a coastal migration of sorts, it is still considered a local move when compared to the great journey that is made by fish from Maryland and Virginia. In a real sense, all these waters are part of the estuarine system of the Hudson River.

During the recent decline of striped bass populations in Chesapeake Bay, the number of fish from this nursery diminished sharply. This had a direct effect on the distance traveled during seasonal migrations by Hudson River fish. With a void left along both north and south shores of Long Island, there was a natural tendency for Hudson River stock to expand into the unclaimed niches. This expansion was further stimulated by exceptionally large and successful year-classes that were produced by the Hudson River population during the late 1980s. They are now contributing more to Long Island's East End fishery than before, and larger numbers are showing up in the Massachusetts fishery. In every population there are always errant wanderers that move beyond their normal ranges. Tag returns of Hudson River fish now come from as far away as Nova Scotia.

In late September and October, the coastal stock of migratory fish begin a southward movement, spurred on by falling temperatures and shifting food-fish populations. The bass school and move southward along New England, west across Long Island, and south along the coast of New Jersey, Delaware and Virginia. Many younger fish return to Chesapeake Bay to winter in lower parts, but large numbers, composed mostly of older bass,

choose to winter in deeper coastal rivers and bays en route or in an area off North Carolina and Virginia. These fish were first discovered there in the early 1980s.

When water temperatures fall below 40 degrees, bass in their various winter locations restrict their movement and enter a somewhat dormant stage. The exception are smaller striped bass, fish one to three years old. They have been shown to actively feed and move about the bays even under the ice. At this time, their migrations are strictly of a feeding nature. During most of the months of December, January and February, they will feed along the edge of deep water. When temperatures rise during the day they will move into shallower water, only to return when temperatures again fall.

The striped bass of North Carolina separate themselves somewhat like the large and small fish of Chesapeake Bay. However, here the separation is even greater geographically. The smaller striped bass will remain in Albemarle Sound during the winter, while larger fish move out the inlets to join wintering fish off the Outer Banks.

—*Nick Karas*

Striped Bass
EQUIPMENT

STRIPED BASS EQUIPMENT

TACKLE

I t is important for any fisherman to be armed with balanced tackle that is suited for the particular species he is after. Just as the muskie angler wouldn't use bluegill tackle, the striped bass fisherman would not troll with an outfit designed for blue marlin.

Knowing what baits to use for stripers is important if you want to catch bass, but equally important is learning what gear to use. Here's what you will need.

Rods & Reels

Balanced tackle—in which rod, reel and line are all in reasonable proportion to one another—is important for a number of reasons. For one, a properly balanced outfit—for example, a 7-foot popping rod with a good conventional reel loaded with 15-pound-test line—is a joy to use. Besides the casting advantage, properly balanced gear makes hooking and playing fish easier and more effective.

Let's take a look at some salt water tackle and how to match it up for striped bass fishing.

Trolling Tackle

Trolling reels have no casting features (such as anti-backlash devices), since their sole function is trolling. Spools are smooth-running, usually operating on ball bearings. The reels are ruggedly built and, of course, corrosion resistant. Unique features include lugs on the upper part of the sideplate for attachment of a big-game harness worn by the fisherman, and a U-shaped clamp for more secure union of rod and reel.

The most important feature on a trolling reel is the drag. If the reel is to handle sizzling runs, its drag must operate smoothly at all times. The drag must not overheat or it may bind, causing the line to break.

Knowing what baits to use for stripers is important. Equally important, however, is learning what gear works best for you.

In most reels the drag is of the star drag type and consists of a series of alternating metal and composition (or leather) washers. Some high-end reels have not one but two drag controls. One is a knob-operated device that lets you preset drag tension to a point below the breaking strength of the line being used. The other is a lever, mounted on the sideplate, that has a number of positions and permits a wide range of drag settings, from very light to the safe maximum for the line in use. This lever, when backed off all the way, throws the reel into free spool.

Trolling reel spools can be made of graphite composites or metal, usually anodized aluminum. Some trolling reels are designed especially for wire and lead-core lines. They have narrow but deep spools and extra-strong gearing.

Trolling Rods

Trolling rods have the strength and fittings to withstand the power of big fish. Most of these rods are built of fiberglass and graphite. Nearly all blue-water rods have a butt section and a tip section—that is, they seldom have ferrules fitted midway along the working length of the rod. In most rods, the tip section is about 5 feet long, while the butts may vary from 14 to 27 inches.

Trolling rods are rated according to the line-strength classes of the International Game Fish Association. The nine IGFA classes for striped bass are 2-pound line, 4-pound line, 6-pound line, 8-pound line, 12-pound line, 20-pound line, 30-pound line, 50-pound line and 80-pound line.

The striped bass fisherman need not concern himself with such a heavy arsenal. He needs only trolling rods in either the 20-pound or 30-pound class. I carry both 20- and 30-pound outfits and invariably use the 20-pound rods. Most experienced fisherman have scaled back their tackle over the years. A decade or so ago, I loaded my 30-pound outfits with 40-pound-test line. I figured I needed that edge if I hooked a big bass. I no longer feel it is necessary, and I rarely lose a good-size fish on 20-pound tackle.

I also use the same balanced tackle for wire line. Most reels will handle 100 yards of wire with 30-pound monofilament backing. The only change I would make would be in the rod. I would pick a rod with good tungsten-carbide guides and tiptop. I have never found a need for roller guides with wire line.

Casting and Boat Rods

I prefer conventional (revolving-spool) reels over spinning tackle for most boat-fishing situations for stripers. I carry two outfits, a popping rod for casting lures and a medium-weight boat rod for deep jigging, live-lining bait and chunking.

The popping rod has a light action, measures 6 to 7 feet and will cast lures from $1/2$ to 1 ounce. This rod is actually a spinoff from the typical fresh water plug rod. The only difference is that a popping rod has a longer straight grip and not the pistol grip. The longer grip makes casting and fighting fish easier. I use a fresh water model level-wind casting reel. Select a reel, however, that will handle at least 250 yards of 14-pound-test line. This popping outfit will be a joy to use on stripers. It will handle all lures up to one ounce. It is perfect for working an inshore bass blitz with plugs, bucktails or jigs.

For live-lining bait or eels, I switch to a heavier boat rod about 6- to 8-feet long that's rated for $3/4$- to three-ounce lures. There is a wide range of light to medium salt water reels that can be matched to this rod. I prefer 20- to

30-pound-test line for this kind of bait fishing and deep jigging.

Big Al Wutkowski, a New Jersey striper expert, also uses rods of this type for live-lining bait. Al uses 30-pound-test line and no leader. He simply ties a treble hook directly to his line, lip- hooks a live bunker or herring and casts into the jetties. He leaves his reel in free-spool with the clicker on. There's no mistaking that first run, but Al waits until the second run, giving the stripers enough time to turn the bait around and eat it headfirst, before setting the hook.

Like Al, I prefer conventional gear for this kind of fishing. The tackle is easier to handle and it gives you more control when fighting a big bass.

Spinning Tackle

Spinning tackle became popular in America in the late 1940s. The reels are unique because the spool remains stationary (does not revolve) when the angler is casting and retrieving. In operation, the weight and momentum of the lure or bait being cast uncoils the line from the reel spool. Unlike conventional revolving-spool reels, in which the momentum of the turning spool can cause backlashes, the spinning reel has no such problem, for the line stops uncoiling at the end of the cast.

The beginner can learn to use spinning gear much faster than he can master conventional tackle and this is likely one of the major reasons spinning tackle has found its way on most boats. It's easy to use and cast from cramped quarters. On a crowded boat, a fisherman can use an underhand cast without endangering anyone. I carry a couple of spinning rods on my boat because they are quick and easy to use by everyone on board without any fear of backlashes.

I use medium-weight spinning tackle and a two-handed 7- to 8-foot rod with a spinning reel that will handle about 300 yards of 15- to 20-pound-test line. I keep two spinning rods handy, one rigged with a bucktail and another with a topwater plug. When a friend unfamiliar with conventional tackle grabs a spinning rod, I have no fear of spending an hour untangling a backlash.

Terminal Tackle

The accessories are as important as links in a chain, so buy the best you can afford. A well-constructed snap swivel of the correct size, for example, won't literally come apart at the seams under the surge of a good strike from a cow bass.

Swivels

Swivels come in many forms and sizes, but basically consist of two or three round metal eyes connected in such a way that each eye can rotate freely and independently of the others. Swivels perform such functions as preventing or reducing line twist, enabling the fisherman to attach much more than one component (sinker and bait, for example) to his line, and facilitating lure changes.

Sinkers

Sinkers, like swivels, come in many shapes and weights. Usually made of lead, they are used to get a bait (or lure) down to the desired depth. Use as light a sinker as possible to get the job done. If you're a surf fisherman and you want to hold bottom, use a pyramid sinker, a shape designed to dig in and hold in sand. If you're drifting bait, however, you will want to use a bank or egg sinker. It's less apt to snag or hang up in the rocks. Trolling leads have swivels at both ends to keep your line from twisting. Learning the purpose behind each design of terminal gear will make it easy for you to come up with the right rig.

Floats or Bobbers

Floats or bobbers, for example, are lighter-than-water devices that are attached to the line. They keep a bait at a predetermined distance above the bottom and signal the strike of a fish. Floats are usually made of cork or plastic. A cork attached on your leader will also keep your bait away from crabs and make it more visible to a cruising striper. Or, if you are having difficulty detecting a strike when live-lining a herring or bunker, attach a cork 6 to 8 feet above your live bait. When the cork goes under and stays under, set the hook!

Hooks

Modern hook design and manufacture have come a long way since the first Stone Age bone hooks, which date back to 5000 B.C.

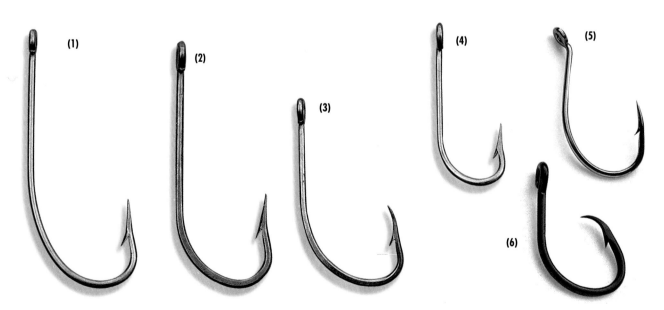

HOOK TYPES for striped bass include (1) Sproat, (2) O'Shaughnessy, (3) Beak, (4) Kirby, (5) Live bait and (6) Circle .

Today's fishhooks come in hundreds of sizes, shapes and special designs. They're hardened and tempered, then plated or bronzed to meet special specifications. Some are thin steel wire for tying salt water flies; others are thick steel for fishing big baits for big fish. There is no such thing as an all-purpose hook.

Fishermen must carry a variety of patterns and sizes to match both tackle and size of fish being hunted. Let's start from the beginning by learning the basic nomenclature of a typical fishing hook (right). Even the various parts of a typical fishhook may vary in design to meet certain requirements. There are sliced or barbed shanks to better hold bait on the hook, forged shanks for greater strength, and so on.

Attempts have been made to standardize hook sizes, but none have been very successful. The problem has been that a hook actually has two measurements—the gap and the length of the shank, both of which vary from pattern to pattern. The correct shank length depends on the type of fishing you plan to undertake. A short shank is preferred for live-lining a bunker or herring or fishing a bunker chunk in the surf, since the hook can be hidden in the bait more easily. The long shank hook is at its best when used for fish with sharp teeth. A bluefish, for example, would have a tough time getting past a long shank and cutting into your leader.

In addition to size and shank length, there are other characteristics of hooks to consider when selecting a hook for a specific purpose. The barb, obviously, is a critical part of the hook. A short barb is quick to set in the mouth of a fish, but it also gives a jumping fish a greater chance of dislodging it. A long barb, on the other hand, is more difficult to set but also makes it a lot tougher for a fish to shake it loose.

So what guidelines should an angler follow? Here are some basic recommendations. The all-round salt water fisherman can't go wrong by using the favorites such as the O'Shaughnessy, Kirby, Sproat and Beak hooks with a barbed shank to hold bait and seaworms up on the shank. Several manufacturers, including Tru-Turn and Owner, have introduced some new innovative hooks worth checking out. Familiarize yourself with the

Parts of a Hook

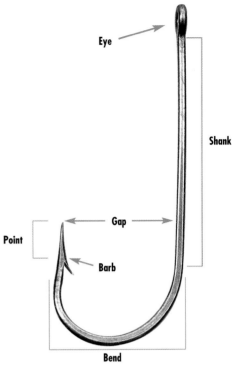

Hook Sizes

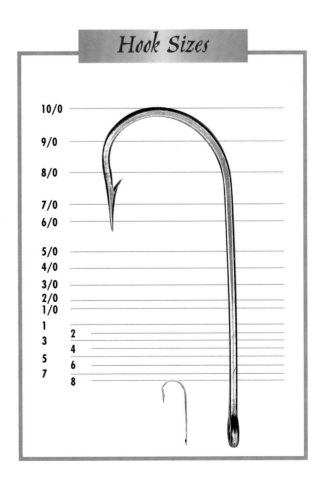

patterns available and compare the differences. It is not difficult to choose the correct size and pattern for your type of fishing. For nearly all types of striped bass fishing in the Northeast, hooks ranging from 2/0 to 8/0 will work under most conditions.

A different style of hook for use with chunk or live bait (as compared to the traditional "J" hooks described above) called the circle hook has recently entered the recreational fishing arena, and is finding favor with more and more striped bass anglers. Circle hooks have been used by commercial fishermen for decades as they are extremely efficient, but the added advantage is that this style invariably hooks the fish in the corner of the mouth, affording easier, unharmed release.

Here's how a circle hook works. A fish will take the bait into its mouth—maybe even swallow it—and start to swim off. The angler merely allows the line to come tight against the rod and pre-set reel drag, and does not try to set the hook in the conventional manner. The hook and bait will be pulled out from the fish's throat and the eye of the hook will actually clear the mouth, but then the hook will rotate and the barb will set itself in the corner of the jaw. It's a simple, near-foolproof technique that virtually eliminates gut- or throat-hooking, and the hook can quickly be removed with a pair of pliers or a de-hooking device.

Sizes for circle hooks differ from those of "J" hooks and can even vary among manufacturers, so you may need to actually visit a tackle shop and look these hooks over to determine the size that's best for the fish you're targeting.

CIRCLE HOOKS are not set like standard hooks. Instead, the angler allows the bass to swallow the bait and swim away. As the fish swims away, the tension on the line pulls the hook out of the fish's throat (1) and as the hook's eye clears the striper's mouth, the hook rotates, which positions the barb (2) so it penentrates the corner of the mouth.

Fishing Lines

Monofilament

No fisherman is stronger than the line that connects him and his fish. Lines are made of a wide variety of natural and synthetic materials and as a result differ widely in their characteristics. Monofilament, for example, has a relatively high rate of stretch, up to 30 percent when wet. Dacron, on the other hand, has 10 percent stretch whether wet or dry.

The most popular line for striper fishermen is monofilament. It's comparatively inexpensive, a factor when you are loading several big salt water reels every season, and it's nearly invisible in water.

Braided Dacron

Dacron is a DuPont trademark for a synthetic fiber that is made into a braided line. It is nearly as strong as monofilament but does not stretch as much (about 10 percent). It has virtually the same characteristics whether wet or dry. Its visibility in water is greater than that of monofilament. Dacron's widest use is as trolling line.

Wire

Wire lines are designed for deep trolling. They're made of stainless steel or Monel (nickel alloy). Because wire is heavy enough to sink on its own, it frequently eliminates the need for a cumbersome trolling drail. Since it has no stretch, the fisherman can also jig the rod and give movement to the bait or lure. However, wire is somewhat tricky to use until a fisherman gets accustomed to it. Kinks can develop, causing weak spots or possibly cutting an angler's hand.

"Super" Braids

The comparatively new high-tech synthetic braided lines get a high score, but you had better listen to sound advice on knots. There are more than a dozen manufacturers of these space-age lines, and they all claim their lines are three times as strong as monofilament of the same diameter. This means, of course, that you can get three times as much line on your reel. The smaller diameter also means easier casting with lighter lures.

Braided lines have a stretch factor of less than 5 percent. Monofilament has a stretch factor of up to 30 percent. This means braided lines will give you more sensitivity and fast hook-ups.

So where's the rub? It's in the knots. With many braided lines, you may only get about 75 percent knot strength and that's only if you use the right knot.

Berkley, a line manufacturer that has done a great deal of research on braided lines, recommends the palomar knot and the Trilene knot. These knots are used to tie fishing line to swivels, snaps, hooks and lures. It's extremely important to wet braided lines before cinching the knot tight and to double the length of the tag line. Some anglers will also secure their knots with one of the superglues.

Braided lines have a lot going for them, including small diameters, minimal stretch and sensitivity.

Fluorocarbon

Fluorocarbon is a synthetic that is much less visible in the water and more durable and abrasion-resistant than monofilament. Fluorocarbon is second to none when it comes to invisibility in the water. It also has reduced "memory" and is extra soft, which gives it good casting characteristics. Fluorocarbon is also relatively expensive, which is one reason many fishermen use it for leader material rather than fishing line. However, the price of fluorocarbon line has dropped significantly since its introduction in the early 1990s.

—*Vin T. Sparano*

KNOTS

nyone who aspires to become a fishing expert must have at least a basic knowledge of knots. Most anglers know and use no more than half a dozen knots. However, if you fish a lot, you are sure to run into a situation that cannot be solved efficiently with the basic knots. The purpose of this section is to acquaint you with the knots that will help you handle nearly all situations.

All knots reduce—to a greater or lesser degree, depending on the knot you use—the breaking strength of the line. Loose or poorly tied knots reduce line strength even more. For that reason, and to avoid wasting valuable fishing time, it is best to practice tying the knots at home. In most cases, it's better to practice with a cord or rope; the heavier material makes it easier to follow the tying procedures.

It is important to form and tighten knots correctly. They should be tightened slowly and steadily for the best results. It helps to moisten the loose knot with saliva from your mouth before tightening the knot. In most knots requiring the tier to make turns around the standing part of the line, at least five such turns should be made.

—*Vin T. Sparano*

Arbor Knot

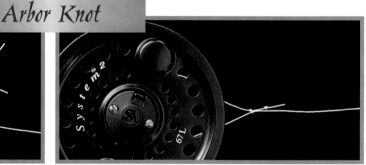

WRAP LINE OR BACKING around spool, then tie tag end of backing around standing line with overhand knot. Tie second overhand knot (arrow) in tag end.

TIGHTEN KNOT in tag end and then pull standing line until knot tightens securely against arbor. Keep pulling until knot in tag end snugs up against main knot.

DOUBLE ABOUT 6 INCHES OF LINE (1) and pass through the eye of the hook. (2) Tie a simple overhand knot in the doubled line, letting the hook hang loose. Avoid twisting the lines. (3) Pull the end of the loop down, passing it completely over the hook. (4) Pull both ends of the line to draw up the knot.

Palomar Knot

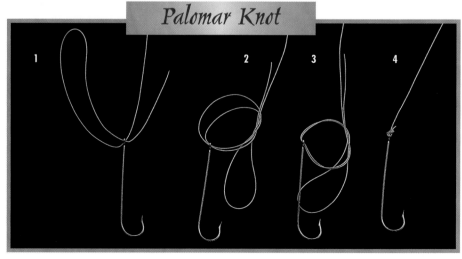

Perfection Loop Knot

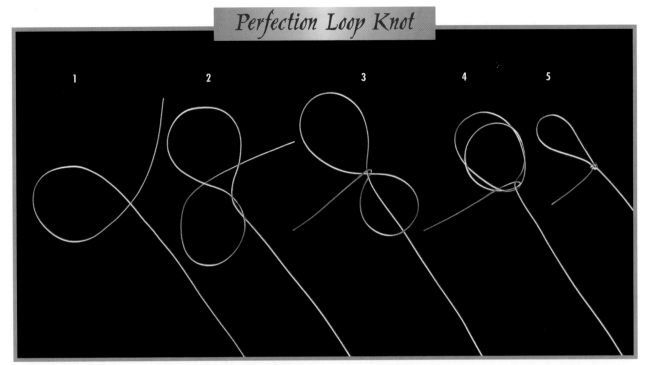

FORM A LOOP (1) in leader by passing tag end behind standing line, tag facing right. Form a second loop (2) in front of first by passing tag end around and then behind first loop. Pass tag end (3) between first two loops; hold tag end to left side. Pull second loop (4) through first loop from behind. Tighten knot (5) by pulling on loop and standing line. Tag should be at right angle to standing line. Trim tag closely.

Dropper Loop Knot

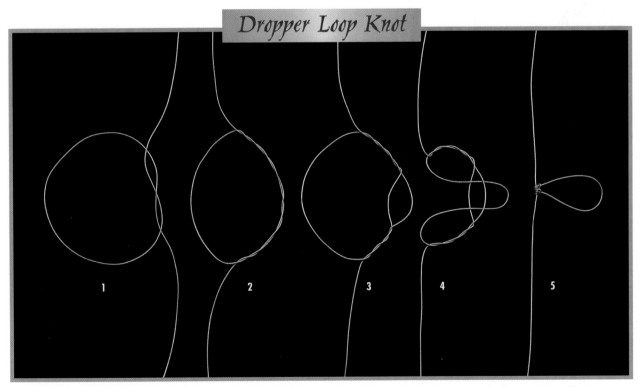

TIE A DROPPER LOOP KNOT by (1) making an overhand knot where you want to form the loop. (2) Pass the free end through the overhand knot five more times. (3) Form an opening halfway between the six wraps. (4) Push the loop through the opening, (5) then pull on both ends of the line to snug up the knot.

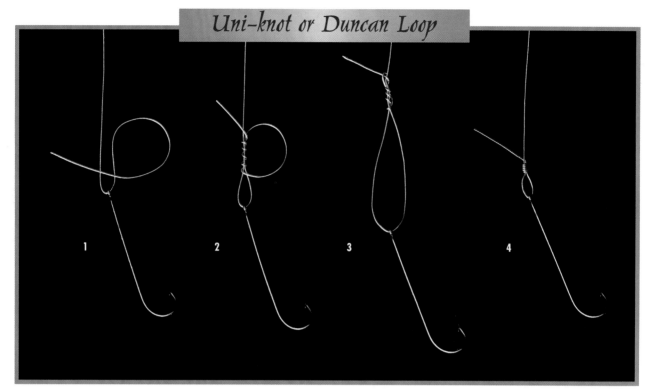

Uni-knot or Duncan Loop

PASS END OF LINE (1) through hook. Form loop in tag end, as shown. Pass tag end through loop (2). Wind tag end through loop and around standing line four times, winding away from hook. Pull tag end (3) to snug up knot. Slide knot (4) to desired position by pulling on standing line. Trim tag.

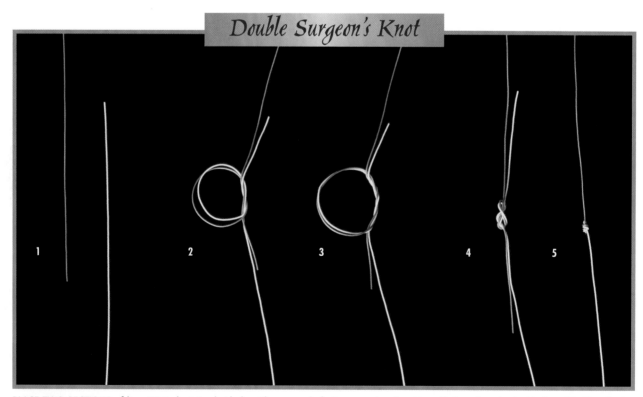

Double Surgeon's Knot

PLACE TWO SECTIONS of line (1) to be joined side by side, tag ends facing opposite directions. Make a loop in double line (2). Pass both ends of line on right (3) through loop to form an overhand knot. Pass same ends through loop a second time (4) to form double overhand knot. Tighten knot (5) by pulling all four ends slowly and evenly. Trim tag ends close to knot.

STRIPED BASS EQUIPMENT

Double Surgeon's Loop

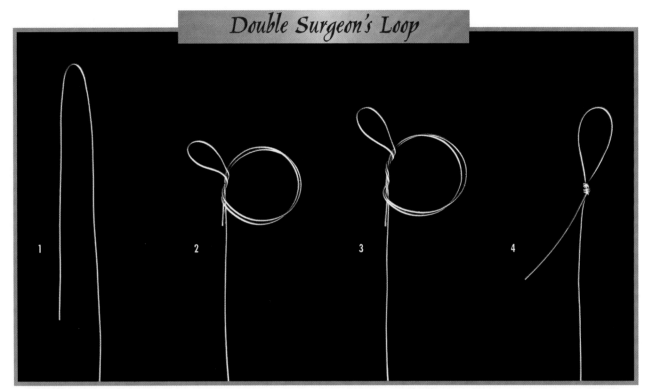

DOUBLE UP (1) the last 6 inches of the leader. Make a loose overhand knot in double line (2). Pass loop end (3) through knot a second time to form double overhand knot. Tighten (4) by holding loop while pulling standing line and tag end until snug. Trim tag closely.

Blood Knot

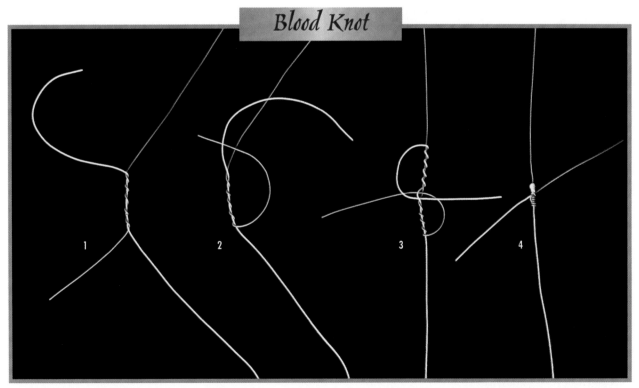

CROSS THE TWO SECTIONS of line to be joined and wrap one tag end around standing part of other line five to seven times (1), depending on line diameter. Pass tag end back between the two lines (2). Wrap other tag end (3) around other standing line five to seven times. Pass tag through same opening as first, in opposite direction. Pull standing lines (4) to tighten knot. Trim tags closely.

Fishing STRATEGIES

FINDING STRIPED BASS

From ocean shorelines to rivers and bays, you'll find the adaptable striper.

ew fish are more universally distributed in inshore waters than the striped bass. From ocean shorelines out to several miles offshore and also in bays and rivers, there's hardly anyplace that you won't find stripers at some time. No fish is better adapted to a wide range of conditions, able to instantly switch from salt to fresh water and vice versa and capable of flourishing in waters so polluted that few other species except eels live in the same environment. Finding stripers is often no big deal, but catching the sizes you're interested in is something else altogether.

Though striped bass are now found throughout the country in landlocked situations, the coastal stripers we're interested in are very mobile, need lots of food and are likely to be found where significant quantities of bait reside.

Fortunately, this is also a very adaptable species that will make do with what's available. For instance, stripers summering along the

Jersey shore will gravitate to live bait such as menhaden when available, but in the absence of such goodies will root calico crabs out of the sand until their jaws become red from abrasion. Fortunately, our search can often be narrowed because stripers are also attracted to structure such as rocks, ledges, wrecks and bars. During migratory periods in the spring and fall, it's possible to run into bass almost anywhere in inshore waters, but during most of the season it's necessary to concentrate on that structure in order to score consistently.

Rips

One of the best places to find stripers on a consistent basis is in a rip. A sharp rise in the bottom with deeper water on both sides creates agitated water during periods of strong current flow, particularly when the wind is in the opposite direction. Rips are instantly recognizable under such circumstances, and are an ideal place for the beginning boater or one without much in the way of electronics to start.

Most of what you have to know is obvious, though a depth finder will help pick out particularly productive portions of the rip or areas just ahead of it. Loran or GPS is also helpful and can be almost a necessity in fog when shore ranges can't be used.

As long as you understand why the bass are there, it will be easy to determine what must be done. Stripers, like human beings, go where the pickings are easy. If someone scattered $100 over a square mile, you'd have to work hard in order to find even a few bucks, and the time and energy expended might not be worth the effort. Yet, if the same $100 were placed in a pile and blown in your direction, a large quantity of the bills could be collected fairly efficiently. That's exactly why stripers pile up on a rip instead of running all over the ocean after baitfish which have plenty of room to escape. By stemming the current just ahead of a rip, bass can simply dart a short distance to grab smaller fish being swept uphill.

Striper stomach contents usually reveal a variety of small fish, as rips provide opportunistic feeding situations and bass are rarely fussy when having to make instant decisions. If there are large rocks on the bottom ahead of the rip, trollers should pay particular attention to working there since stripers can both utilize

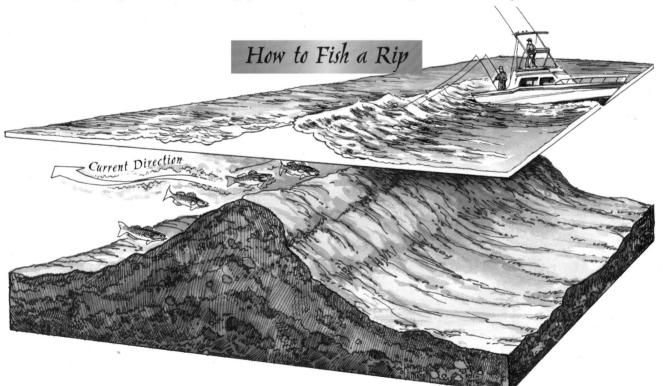

How to Fish a Rip

Current Direction

POSITION YOUR BOAT just in front of the rip's white water. Maintain your position by applying enough power to stay in front of the rip's standing wave. Present your lure or bait to the active fish, which will be set up in front of or on top of the lip.

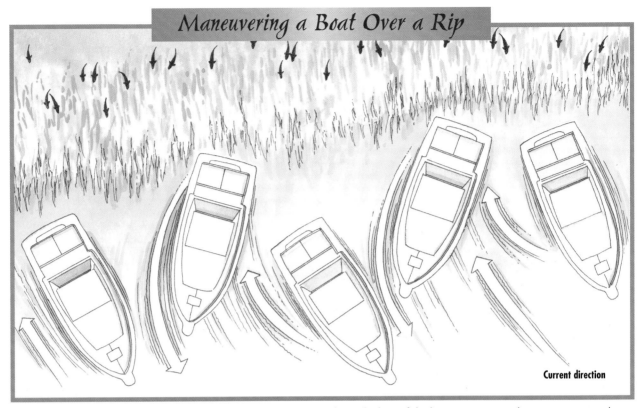

Current direction

CHANGE POSITION ON A RIP by "crabbing" the boat. Increase power and turn the bow of the boat crossways to the current, moving the boat in that direction. After moving over, straighten the boat and decrease the power to maintain a line on the rip.

them as hiding places and save even more energy by not having to fight the current as much. Many northern rips, such as those at Montauk, Long Island and Cuttyhunk, Massachusetts, have rough bottoms with rocks and mussel beds. Others, such as Monomoy and the Nantucket rips in Massachusetts, as well as Sandy Hook, New Jersey, and the many rips at the mouth of Delaware Bay, are sandy.

Tide can make a big difference in any rip, and local knowledge is important in that respect. Flood tides are often preferred in the spring when bait is moving inshore, but the ebb seems to be the favorite of most rip specialists. That's especially the case in the fall as young-of-the-year fish of many kinds migrate out to sea before heading for warmer waters.

The basics of trolling any rip are universal, though each has its peculiarities. Some lazy bass may feed in back of the rip, but most set up a feeding station ahead of it or almost on top. Thus, the angler should maintain a distance ahead of the white water which enables him to troll his lure at that lip or just ahead. This is accomplished by utilizing barely enough power to maintain headway. As the boat moves a bit farther ahead of the rip to cover deeper water, the skipper turns his bow slightly sideways to the current, which shifts him back into the proper position again a bit further up on the rip. This procedure, which I refer to as "crabbing" (just as a crab scuttles sideways), allows you to cover the entire rip.

After getting to the end of the rip, let your lure wash into deeper water before either shifting the bow to cover it in the other direction or picking up and running back to the starting point. I've had success going both ways, but in many cases that's impossible if others are working the rip below you. In some areas everyone works in only one direction. For instance, at the Sandy Hook rip in central New Jersey, directly across from New York City, the run is from the outside (eastern) end to the shallower inner portion nearer shore. In most cases wire line is used to troll lures at a set depth on rips, but the shallower rips, such as Sandy Hook, can also be worked with swimming plugs on mono—particularly if deep-diving plugs are utilized.

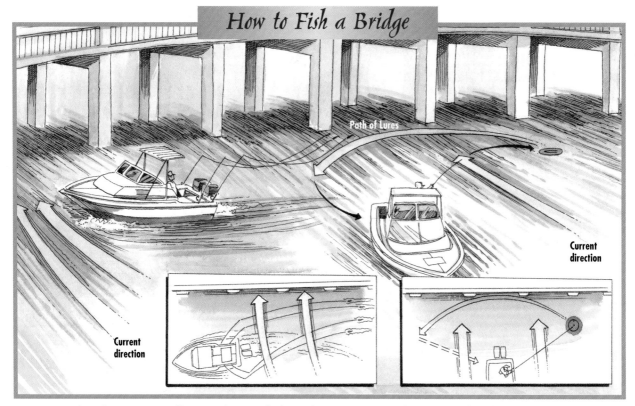

Path of Lures

Current direction

Current direction

Current direction

FISH BRIDGES by either casting or trolling. In either case the lure or bait must pass very close to the bridge pilings. When casting, throw the lure or bait past the piling you want to fish so it swings into or near it.

Rips can also be fished with bait. Indeed, some rips have become so saturated with boaters drifting seaworms or eels that trolling is often almost impossible. Diamond, bucktail or plastic-tail jigs are also drifted through rips, and a more specialized technique involves stemming the current, just as when trolling and dropping a jig back into the current until it's behind the rip. That technique involves a lot of reeling, as you get only two or three bounces off bottom in a fast current before having to retrieve, but it's a good way to operate when the rip is rough. Bait fishing a rip from anchor is gaining in popularity, especially among those using bunker (menhaden) chunks at Montauk.

Rips "make up" best when the wind is against the current, yet that is also when they're most dangerous to drift through. Many a boater has lost his life in those crashing waves, and it's imperative that the utmost caution be exercised. However, as skilled boaters soon recognize, the wind-against-current situation that results in big seas at the edge of the rip also creates an area of smooth water with only a swell just ahead of it. Thus, it's safe to troll or power jig into the rip even in a howling wind against current as long as you stay above the rip and fight hooked bass back to you, rather than drift through to try to make the fight easier.

Bridges

Bridges provide another obvious form of structure which almost always harbor stripers at some stage of the tide. Whether fishing the Golden Gate in San Francisco Bay, the Chesapeake Bay Bridge-Tunnel or much smaller bridges such as those connecting Long Island with Jones Beach, the fundamentals are similar. Stripers will be facing into the current for easy pickings, and the boater must troll, drift or cast to place lure or bait within easy reach of them. Some surface action may be available, but by and large it's necessary to get down near bottom in order to catch the most and the largest stripers.

Straight wire line trolling works well, especially where pilings are set far apart,

EXPERIMENT WITH YOUR PRESENTATION on a rough shoreline. You can cast its entire length (1), covering every little pocket of water, or slow-troll just offshore (2), which covers a lot of water. Drifting downwind (3) is another way to present your bait.

though many bridge trollers employ weights so they can work with shorter lines, which are more easily manuevered around pilings without hanging up.

Rocky Shorelines

Another sure bet for stripers is rocky shorelines, which boaters can work by trolling just offshore (beware of underwater rocks and tide stages that can leave such rocks barely covered) or casting with plugs and eels. Long Island Sound is one area loaded with such structure where anglers trolling worms at a snail's pace do very well with schoolies, while those drifting or slow-trolling live bunkers score with jumbos.

Inlets

Inlets are another place where stripers will gather at times. In fact, they'd probably be there all the time if it wasn't for boat traffic. Smaller inlets are virtually impossible to fish during the day from a boat, and night is the best bet almost everywhere except during migratory periods. An added complication involves anglers casting from inlet jetties, which often prevents boaters from getting to the best portions of the inlet. Since those fishermen are much more restricted in what they can do, sportsmanship requires that boaters stay out of shore fishermen's range. Live bait is a good bet in inlets, as eels, bunker, herring and worms can be drifted through with the tide. As a general rule, the ebb is preferred since it's easiest for stripers to nail baitfish sucked out to them in the narrow and often rough inlet mouth.

Bottom Types

Most structure isn't as obvious as it is in rips, at bridges, among exposed rocks and in inlets. Stripers are much more likely to concentrate over rough bottoms, around wrecks, and on edges of channels rather than on sand simply because these areas are more attractive to many forms of marine life. If small bait isn't coming through, bass can always forage on

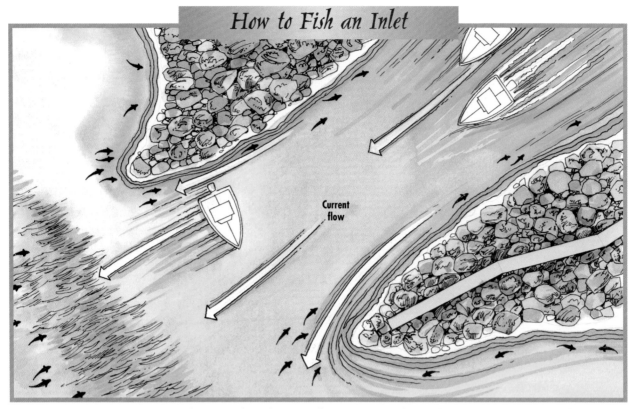

DRIFTING ALONG WITH AN EBB TIDE at the mouth of an inlet can produce some outstanding catches. However, heavy boat traffic can limit the number of fish present. Give the right-of-way to shore-bound anglers casting from jetties.

bottom for crabs, lobsters and whatever else might be edible.

Local knowledge is important in determining where those good bottoms are, though many can be picked up on fishing charts of the area. With Loran and GPS to work with, even beginners can soon have a list of "hot" numbers without having to worry about ranges or any "sixth sense."

Elevated rocky bottoms in areas where most of the surrounding territory is sandy are good bets for stripers. Shrewsbury Rocks off the northern New Jersey shore is an example of such a spot that attracts all sorts of marine life and concentrates predators, which don't have many good alternatives in the area.

Mussel bottoms seem to be particularly effective for bunker chunking, and there's so much bottom like this in areas such as Raritan Bay, between Staten Island and northern New Jersey, that it's often possible to anchor up far from well-known spots and catch bass steadily all by yourself in one of the country's most heavily fished areas.

Night is usually preferred to day, especially for trolling and when big bass rather than schoolies are desired. However, trolling at night on the dark of the moon isn't usually productive during the summer and early fall due to phosphoresence in warmer waters, which lights up both line and lure to make the latter appear unrealistic. Thus, the period from half moon to the full and down again to half provides the best night trolling, since there's little or no phosphoresence under such circumstances.

Stripers rarely bite throughout a tide, and may only hit at certain stages. While working Shagwong Reef at Montauk during the night, I found that the middle of the ebb was usually best off the full moon, as that's when currents were strongest. Yet during the few days around the full moon, it was exactly the opposite, as bass tended to hit at the beginning and end of the tide, while the middle would often be dead in the extremely hard flow. Yet there were so many exceptions to that rule that I almost always simply fished the entire ebb as long as it was entirely in the dark.

—*Al Ristori*

BAIT FISHING

Stripers will take a wide variety of natural baits. The secret lies in the rigging and presentation of your offering.

Since stripers eat virtually anything edible at some time during their lives, it would take a book to merely scratch the surface of every bait-fishing technique employed by boaters around the country. However, the discussion of various bait types should cover others of similar size that may be employed by anglers in areas where I don't have personal familiarity with the fishing. For instance, nose- or jaw-hooking a live anchovy in San Francisco Bay or a peanut bunker (baby menhaden) along the Jersey shore amount to about the same thing.

Some of the techniques discussed will be peculiar to a particular area, but in most cases they can be utilized in other areas with similar baits if an angler wants to put in the time to experiment. Consider that dead anchovies are a prime bait for striped bass in Lake Mead, Nevada, and it should be obvious that stripers aren't much different no matter where they're found. When they're targeting a specific baitfish, such as abundant alewives in a lake or sand eels off the northeast coast, it may be hard to distract them except with those baits or lures that resemble the forage. However, if there's no such abundant attraction, bass will usually feed on whatever's available.

Striper fishermen reading this chapter in the future will probably wonder why I ignored *their* favorite bait fishing technique. The fact of the matter is that there are infinite variations even to this most basic technique. As this is written, the most popular and effective means of catching bass at Montauk, where bass have long been the major species, is bunker chunking. Yet while that technique was utilized for some time in Long Island Sound, anchoring forward of Montauk rips to practice the sport only came into practice during the 1990s. Even as this is written, bunker chunking still isn't practiced in many other areas of the coast where the raw material is readily available. To anglers in those areas, this will be a revolutionary technique when it catches on.

Menhaden

At every life stage, there's probably nothing more desirable or commonly available to stripers than the menhaden, or bunker. Better known in New England as pogy (not to be confused with the scup, which is called porgy in the Mid-Atlantic) and in North Carolina as fatback, bunkers are the oiliest fish around. Large purse seiners catch them in huge quantities for reduction to fish oil and meals. Smaller seiners take millions of pounds for both crab and lobster bait and for use by sport fishermen as everything from ground-up chum to chunking material and whole or strip baits for sharks and giant tuna.

There's a world of difference between fresh-dead and frozen bunkers. The fresh bunker has a slime that is particularly attractive to game fish along with a sheen and reddish meat that virtually exudes oils. The frozen product loses the slime and sheen, and has whitish flesh which falls apart easily.

Always opt for fresh bunkers whenever possible, but don't write off the frozen baits, which can work just as well when stripers are turned on. Indeed, I've often worked a hook into a solidly frozen chunk and gotten a strike immediately upon reaching bottom.

Rigs are pretty basic. A variety of hooks from 3/0 to 7/0 can be used as long as they have sufficient strength to hold a 30-pound fish in a boiling current. These can be rigged to a mono or fluorocarbon leader three feet or more in length with a small swivel at the other end. The line is run through a fishfinder, a hollow piece of plastic with a snap or other device to hold the sinker, which allows it to

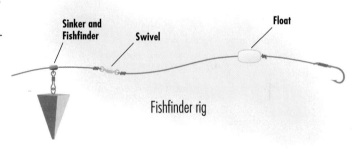

Fishfinder rig

slide along the line so bass can't feel the sinker when they pick up the bait. That's not often critical with a hungry striper, and some anglers use a simple three-way swivel rig instead.

Most fishermen probably credit stripers with being more line-shy than they really are when it comes to bait. To avoid being cut off continually while chunking when bluefish are mixed in, some veterans use black nylon-covered braided wire leaders. Capt. John Alberda, who popularized bunker chunking in Long Island Sound long before it was adopted by others, uses wire leaders for bass, and his results can't be challenged.

Bunker chunking is done from anchor ahead of a rip or bridge, over mussel or rocky bottom or at the edges of channels—in other words, just about anywhere stripers gather over bottom and where there's a current to spread the scent. So attractive is the scent that very little chunking is usually required. Indeed, too much chunking can be a deficit, as it may attract hordes of crabs, or the chunks may be carried so far away from the boat that you're chumming for someone anchored downtide of you.

The best time to start is at the beginning of a tide, so the anchor is stretched in the proper direction and several chunks can be thrown out to "salt" the area. Slow the chunking as the current increases, and throw an occasional piece toward the bow to vary the sink rate. You don't want to have bass stacked up far behind the boat where it's difficult to get to them or set a hook.

Most anglers cut bunkers from top to bottom and get several pieces about an inch or so wide, including the head. Only the tails aren't used as bait since they have relatively little meat and spin in the current when placed on a hook. The next cut up from the tail is also a good candidate for chum, while the portions which include internal organs prove most effective as bait. It's hard to keep the

guts on a hook, so Staten Island pro Tony Arcabascio pulls the heart out and puts that tough organ on the hook ahead of a chunk. Don't throw away the head, as it's the perfect bait if you're trying to avoid smaller bass in order to wait out a larger fish.

The technique is simple, as the rig is merely dropped to bottom with a minimum of weight, and the rod can be stuck in a holder with the reel in click. Since most stripers today are released, use only a very short drop-back in order to prevent gut-hooking. We'll probably see more use of circle hooks in this fishery in order to decrease release mortality.

Just as in big-game fishing, it's essential to reel until the handle can't be turned any longer before striking, as stripers will often run uptide with the bait, and striking against a bow in the line will only warn them to spit it out.

A recent development at Montauk will probably spread to all areas where strong currents are a factor. Rather than using mono or even the new braided lines (such as Berkley Fireline and Spiderwire), which require less sinker weight, wire line is employed to allow a free-fall with little or no weight. Since standard wire is very stiff and difficult to handle in free-spool, braided wire (which doesn't sink quite as well) is employed. Even with mono there are times when it's possible to drift the chunk astern and hook up without being anywhere near bottom, but the odds are much better in the depths. The same method will work with other chunks. Mackerel, herring, squid and any other baitfish available in quantity may do the job, though it's tough to beat the bunker's oil content and subsequent attraction to striped bass and many other species.

Huge numbers of stripers are caught by bunker chunking in such areas as Montauk, Long Island Sound, Raritan Bay and even the lower Hudson River and the southern New England coast. The method is spreading, but

CHOPPED BUNKER for chumming and baiting.

it can produce different results in various areas. Whereas all the aforementioned spots produce lots of 10- to 20-pounders and quite a few thirties at Montauk, there are better methods for jumbos. Yet, when Delaware Bay anglers started bunker chunking in shallow waters close to the South Jersey shore a few years ago, they came up with the largest stripers in the state—up to 60 pounds!

Live bunkers make great baits for jumbo stripers. In contrast to the blind hits in chunking, live bunker fishing is far more exciting, since bass chase the 1- to 2-pound bunkers to the surface and create huge boils while trying to catch up to them. Unfortunately, there's often more excitement than catching involved when stripers miss the big baits or just play with them. In addition, setting the hook with such a large bait is another problem. Some pros favor trebles of various sizes, while others use large single hooks such as a wide-bend 7/0 Siwash. Bunkers are normally hooked through the nose to make for easy casting, though anglers often try other hooking methods when nose-hooking doesn't produce.

Live bunkers can be fished from a drifting boat with a simple short leader rig, though a split shot or light drail may be helpful in windy conditions. Under calm conditions it's often helpful to use a float to keep the bunker high in the water column.

Even fresh-dead whole bunkers will work at times when big stripers are thick. There were several years in the late 1960s when 20- to 60-pound bass were stacked up during early summer off Sandy Hook in such quantities that they could be caught regularly by drifted fresh-dead bunkers. Many boaters obtained their bunkers still alive from pound nets in Sandy Hook Bay, but bunker fishing was so new to most that no one seemed to even make an attempt at keeping them alive to fish just a few miles away on the other side of the Hook. The dead bunkers were so effective that the body of jumbo stripers summering there was quickly wiped out.

As exciting as live bunker fishing can be, it's often ineffective when stripers are lazy. One early fall day a few years ago there were lots of small schools of adult bunkers within a few hundred yards of Point Pleasant Beach, New Jersey, and I ran my boat out to see what might be under them. Snagging bunkers was no problem, but every live bait was only mauled by bluefish. Getting disgusted with my lack of success, I cut one of the chopped bunkers into chunks and put it on a wire-leadered bluefish hook in order to at least

NOSE-HOOKING a live bunker.

hook one of the choppers. It wasn't long after I cast the chunk into a bunker school and let it sink to bottom in about 30 feet that the bait was picked up. To my great surprise, that fish turned out to be a striper in the 20s, and I then caught two more in the same size class before the wind came up and the bunker schools dispersed. Why those bass ignored a live bunker but jumped on chunks was a mystery, though I've seen it happen at other times.

Young-of-the-year bunkers measuring only a few inches are a great attraction for school stripers during the fall as both species migrate south. Anglers refer to those baby menhaden as "peanut bunkers," and they're highly desirable baitfish since the tightly-packed schools tend to stay on the surface and create casting opportunities with flies and popping plugs. Though the adult bunker population had been beaten down to very low levels by 1998 due to extensive purse-seining activity, the spawn that year was outstanding, and peanut bunkers migrated south along the northeast coast in massive quantities, providing anglers with the best surface sport in memory. Not only did those bass have stomachs absolutely stuffed with the baby bunkers, but millions more of the peanuts were cast up by waves on beaches in their desperate attempt to avoid predators. Yet the schools of forage just kept coming right through December.

Catching bunkers when they're available is no problem. Just spot the flipping fish on the surface and cast a weighted treble snag hook into them. Let it sink before retrieving in big sweeps to snag an unseen bait. Resist the temptation to retrieve right away and snag those on the surface. There are always many more under those that are visible. Unless hit in the gills, they can be kept alive easily in a live well as long as they're not crowded. Those intended for chunking should be kept cool, but not directly on ice, which takes the desirable slime off them.

A much easier means of catching lots of bunkers is with a cast net. This can be done by spotting schools and sneaking up on them, or even better, by utilizing your depth finder to mark underwater schools and drop on them. Since peanut bunkers turn the surface purple, they're easy to spot and net, though a much smaller mesh must be used. Those peanuts

make great live baits on light tackle, though few anglers bother with them since stripers almost invariably hit plugs, flies and jigs well when they're feeding on them.

Eels

Cobia, bluefish, white marlin and many other game fish love to eat eels on the rare occasions they happen upon them in nature or when fishermen present them, but no predator is more associated with this bait than the striped bass. Though once considered to be almost exclusively a night bait for stripers, eels also work very well during the day, provided there aren't too many toothy critters around to chop them up.

Boaters can fish eels in a number of ways, with casting and drifting being the most common. Casting is the preferred method within bays and when working into rocks. Some of the most exciting striper sport I ever encountered involved casting eels at night in Pleasant Bay, Massachusetts, where I not only caught the 61-pounder noted earlier but also lots of '30s and '40s. Jimmy Andrews normally anchored along the edges of channels where there was hardly enough water left to float his skiff out at low tide.

We'd cast the entire outgoing tide, reeling the eel back slowly but with enough motion to keep it from heading into the grass. On occasion we'd also drift, but that slow retrieve in narrow channels was hard to beat. Since even big bass tend to nip at the tails of eels under these circumstances, it's usually advisable to give a short drop-back so the bait can be picked up and turned in the striper's mouth. Reel tight and set the hook as soon as line starts moving out steadily. There are nights when bass will crash eels, and you can adjust to striking immediately when that trend starts.

Wherever there are jetties along the coast, casting eels into them is a consistent means of tempting stripers. That's especially the case at night and even in the dog days of summer. However, live bunkers are usually a better bet in the daytime for that sport.

Drifting is a much more common and easier means of working a live eel. Capt. Bob Rocchetta broke the 73-pound standard that had stood since 1913 when he fed an eel to a

76-pound striper in the rips off Montauk during the eclipse of the moon on July 17, 1981.

The fishfinder rig (p. 53) or one fashioned with a three-way swivel does the job, though longer leaders are favored for eels. In rocky areas such as the rips, Great Eastern and Porgy Hump at Montauk plus nearby Plum Gut and The Race, a lighter piece of mono may be used for the sinker so it can be broken off when it hangs up. Rather than letting the

sinker drag and getting hung continuously, the technique involves hitting bottom and reeling up a couple of turns. As the boat approaches the peak you're fishing, keep testing for bottom and shortening up until the recorder shows you dropping down the other side. Then it's necessary to let out some line to keep in contact. Unlike surface rips, underwater hills often produce better on the back side rather than the front. Sturdy boat rods capable of handling sinkers up to eight ounces are utilized, and no drop-back is normally given. Just dip the rod tip on the pick-up and let the line come tight before striking. With a fast current in 30 to 50 feet, stripers simply glomp an eel rather than play with it, as is often the case in quiet bays.

Probably no other group goes through as many eels for bait as anglers fishing the mouth of Delaware Bay. The Cape May rips spread practically from one side of the bay to the other and are loaded with bass from

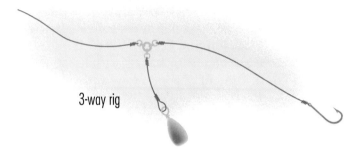

3-way rig

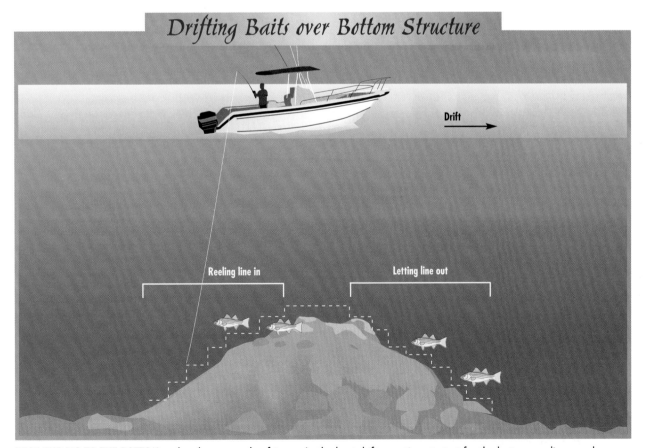

Drifting Baits over Bottom Structure

Drift

Reeling line in

Letting line out

DROP THE RIG TO THE BOTTOM and reel up a couple of turns. As the boat drifts, continue to test for the bottom, reeling up whenever bottom is contacted. When the depthfinder shows you are going down the other side of the hump, let out enough line to maintain contact with the bottom.

October to December. Thousands of anglers from both New Jersey and Delaware converge on the dozens of rips to post some impressive catches by drifting eels. Since these shallow rips are sandy, there's rarely a hang-up, and the technique is basically the same except with lighter gear. Schoolies dominate, so many anglers use light spinning tackle.

Eels are the easiest live bait to handle since they don't even require water. Just keep them wet, cool and out of the sun. At night they can be held in a bucket on deck, though I prefer a killie trap that can be dipped occasionally with the ends plugged. Some provision to maintain moisture and cool temperatures must be made in daylight. If a bucket or other container with holes or a drain at the bottom is available, place ice in it and some sort of barrier above the ice so the eels will stay cool but won't be swimming in ice cold water. The cold will slow them down and make it easier to handle this very slimy bait.

Always have rags available with which to handle eels. Get a firm grip near the head and run a 3/0 to 5/0 hook through the lower jaw and out one eye socket. Eels are usually good for several stripers, though the hook hole may open somewhat, which requires that the hook be shifted to the other eye socket. Even fresh-dead eels work at times, though as a general rule I use them only as long as their tail curls a bit when they're held up.

Never let a hooked eel hang. Either place them in water after hooking or with a bit of slack on the deck, where they'll usually just slither around. If hanging they'll immediately twist up in your leader and it will probably be necessary to unhook them simply to get the slimy mess straightened out. You don't want that to happen when making drops over a hump or in a rip, because after running uptide you'll be sweeping through the payoff zone within seconds of reaching bottom.

A wide variety of eel sizes provide good bait. So-called pencil eels of about 6 to 9 inches are ideal for light tackle and use in shallow bay areas for schoolies. Eels from 9 to 15 inches or more are better for casting with heavier tackle or drifting in deeper waters and faster currents. Even large eels can be sucked in by relatively small stripers in a gulp, so don't be put off by having to use eating-size baits. Remember that bass must swallow any bait headfirst, and your hook is in the head!

Eels can be caught in almost any bay or river with eel pots, then kept for months in flowing water without any attention. Most anglers buy them at tackle shops and marinas, but the resurgence of striped bass and the consequent huge increase in demand for eels as bait results in frequent shortages and ever-increasing prices.

Eels don't make a good dead baits unless action is imparted to them. Several decades

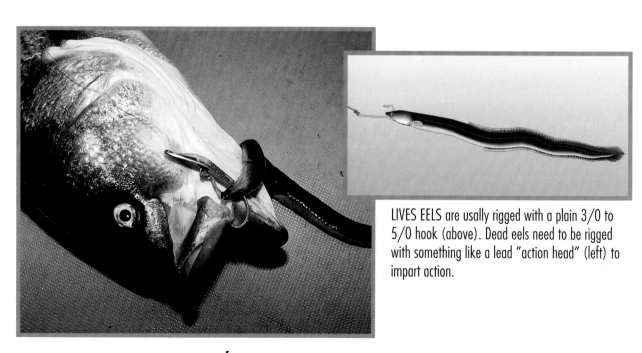

LIVES EELS are usally rigged with a plain 3/0 to 5/0 hook (above). Dead eels need to be rigged with something like a lead "action head" (left) to impart action.

ago the most popular night-trolling lure at Montauk was a dead eel rigged on a lead "action head." Similar rigs are used for casting into jetties by a few pros, and salted eel skins turned inside out to utilize the blue side are also rigged over large swimming plugs to make a trolling or casting lure with irresistible action. Very few anglers use dead eels now, but those willing to go through the skinning and rigging process can keep them for years in jars with a heavy kosher brine solution.

Mackerel

Herring & Alewives

One of the great attractions for striped bass arriving early along the northeast coast during the spring migration are the many herring runs. River herring and alewives start moving into coastal ponds through narrow spillways or flumes a month or more before bass arrive in order to spawn and return to sea. These fish make ideal live baits when fished not only in the immediate vicinity of the spillway but also anywhere else where early-season bass may gather. Some pros collect and store them in large cages sunk in flowing water areas, and a few even erect big pens that can hold thousands long after the runs are over.

Herring are usually hooked through the nose with either a large single hook or a treble, and allowed to swim freely from a drifting boat. Their shape makes them a lot easier for stripers to swallow than adult bunkers, and bass rarely fool with them much before engulfing the slim, silvery fish.

Sea herring are often larger but also make good live baits when available, though that usually involves catching them near where large stripers may be feeding. They can also be chunked just as bunkers are, and make a good substitute if they can be obtained in fresh condition.

Mackerel

The spring migration of these fish passes by too quickly for them to be of any use as live baits in the Mid-Atlantic. However, they are a summer staple in New England north of Cape Cod, where both stripers and mackerel live during the warmer months. A large single or small treble hook worked through the nose allows the mackerel to swim freely for an hour or so on the drift, and they also make an excellent bait for slow trolling.

One summer, when I kept my boat in Montauk, we were able to run over to Block Island's new harbor and jig some mackerel in the channel before rushing back to the Porgy Hump with our precious cargo and dropping them to bottom for instant hook-ups. Though those were large mackerel in the two-pound range, jumbo bass had no trouble inhaling them with no drop-back other than lowering the rod tip. Any baits that died were fished as fillets, which also produced at times.

Since mackerel have no air bladders, they need a lot of room and a circular tank so they can swim continuously. Small boaters on Cape Cod troll or jig a few with mackerel jigging rigs and keep them alive in round galvanized tubs by changing the water regularly. Don't attempt to keep more than a few alive in ordinary live bait wells as they require a lot of room, and you'll lose all of them quickly if crowded.

Squid

Stripers love squid, but that species is rarely available in live form when bass are available, and it doesn't seem to have the same allure when fished as a dead bait. The large inshore runs of squid each spring in northern areas may be a thing of the past, now that there's much greater commercial exploitation of the species. But it was squid moving into Pleasant Bay on Cape Cod during the 1960s that created some of the most exciting action with large stripers I've ever experienced, as jumbos exploded on Reverse Atom plugs. Yet no one even attempted to catch squid for live bait at the time. If you can obtain them, they're not hard to keep alive, and with a hook placed in the tail they'll swim for hours.

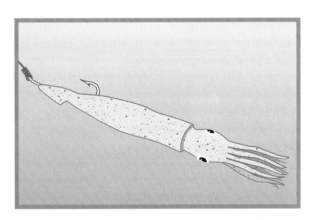

Small Live Baitfish

Just about any small fish will make a meal for a striper—for example, anchovies and sardines in California and bottom fish like tautog (blackfish), pollock and winter flounder in the Northeast. Minimum size laws have made it difficult, if not impossible, to legally use tautog and flounders, but cunners (bergalls, choggies) are an adequate substitute that have no minimum size restriction. Bottom fish are especially effective in inlets and canals where they can be caught on the spot and are a natural food source. Use smaller hooks than with larger baits in order to allow these fish to swim effectively, as all live baits must in order to

attract predators. One might think that predators would favor an easily captured half-dead bait, but that's rarely the case. Most often they'll pass up such an offering, but can be turned on with a lively bait.

Sand Eels

One of the most important natural baits for stripers is rarely used alive and won't last long on even the lightest hook in any case. However, anglers on the bay side of Cape Cod frequently rake these long, slim baitfish out of the sand at night and catch lots of school bass by placing several sand eels on a hook and fishing them dead on bottom.

Seaworms

School stripers love seaworms and frequently won't respond to anything else. Though jumbos rarely bother with them, schoolies respond readily to sandworms, bloodworms, tapeworms and any other species you can dig up or buy. One or two are placed on a light hook (preferably a baitholder-type) at the head and allowed to dangle seductively. Do not bunch them up, as it's essential that they flow naturally behind the hook rather than spinning. Worms are generally drifted with a three-way swivel or fishfinder rig and are especially effective in areas where schoolies concentrate, such as rips. Dropbacks aren't normally needed as even tiny bass strike at the head, and you can hook them by simply lowering the rod tip and then striking.

Clams

Stripers aren't equipped to deal with clams in nature, but they love what's in the shell and gladly respond when that meat becomes available. Nature provides such an occasional bonus every so often along northeastern beaches when easterly storms tear up the bottom and drive surf clams of all sizes ashore. Those not eaten by seagulls die and are washed back into the surf over the course of the next several days to create a free lunch for stripers. The fact that most of those clams smell pretty bad by that point doesn't bother our finned friends at all.

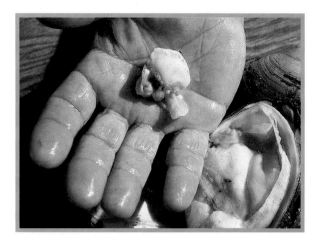

Boaters generally don't fish bass with clams as surfcasters do, but the use of clam bellies for chum and bait is often deadly on schoolies in bays and the mouths of inlets.

Clam processers cut out the bellies, and if cans of them are available there's often no finer bait. Long Island is the only area where tackle shops regularly sell cans of frozen clam bellies. A few bellies are drifted back from an anchored boat, and other bellies are placed on light hooks to be drifted back. Since productive clam belly waters are usually shallow, it's rarely advisable to use any weight, as the belly will quickly fall to bottom where crabs will dine on it instead of bass.

Soft-shell (steamer) clams have long been a favorite striper bait in Chesapeake Bay and were probably the prime summer bait—as well as chum dribbled from anchored boats—when schoolies were super-abundant there in the 1960s.

Grass Shrimp

These tiny crustaceans can be netted or dredged in weedy bays and are another great

bait for school stripers, though they're better known as a weakfish attractor. At anchor, dribble a few at a time around bay channel edges and alongside jetties where the current flow isn't too great. Several grass shrimp can be placed on a light wire hook, or a worm can be substituted as bait in the shrimp chum line. This is a truly natural bait that is often found in school stripers caught in bays.

Crabs & Lobster

Though hard-shell crustaceans aren't high on the striper's list of favorites, they'll eat them when nothing softer is available. Soft-shell blueclaw crabs work very well in Chesapeake Bay both as a direct bait and for tipping jigs in order to give them a scent. Soft-shell calico crabs can be hand-dredged out of Mid-Atlantic surf areas during the summer and make an irresistible bottom bait. Tautog fishermen frequently hook stripers on cut green crabs in the fall, though no one fishes for bass specifically in that fashion. The juvenile spidercrab shown above isn't a common striper bait, but bass certainly eat them on occasion. I doubt if anyone uses lobsters for bait either, but keep in mind that lobsters were used as both chum and bait at the famed Cuttyhunk bass stands during the late 19th century. Menhaden, eels and crabs were also used as chum, but the favored bait was a lobster tail, which would be a pretty expensive bait today!

—*Al Ristori*

LURE FISHING FOR STRIPERS

There's hardly an inshore lure that won't attract stripers at one time or another. Fresh water anglers could probably run through their tackle box and catch schoolies on virtually every lure at some time. Except for such uniquely salt water creations as the bunker spoon, there isn't much of a difference between most fresh water lures and those used in salt water except size and sturdier hooks.

Popping Plugs

Though hardly the most effective lure with which to catch stripers, poppers are my favorites. Any fish that will hit a popper is a thrill to cast to even if the catch isn't completed. The surface strike alone is sufficient compensation for the work involved.

Most anglers utilize standard cup-faced poppers, which are worked with steady jerks of the rod tip to create a splashing action. The Atom Striper Swiper, created by Bob Pond, was one of the first successful post–WW II mass-produced poppers, and there have been many variations of that type over the years.

My personal preference is the pencil popper, a plug with a slim head and fat rear that doesn't pop in the conventional fashion.

POPPING PLUGS such as this pencil popper are effective when fish are feeding on the surface. These lures are not only productive, but a lot of fun.

while expending so little energy that I can cast all day.

Though even non-feeding stripers can sometimes be awakened by the action of a popper, those lures are basically restricted to use when bass are in a surface feeding mode. A moderately fast retrieve is usually best, and while schoolies are the usual quarry, I've caught bass over 40 pounds on poppers in Cape Cod Bay when herring were being chased.

The great wooden lure maker Stan Gibbs created that lure at his Cape Cod shop and taught me how to work it correctly during the 1960s. The Gibbs pencil popper is still made by his successors, and Cotten Cordell later manufactured a hollow plastic version, which is less expensive but still very effective. Yo-Zuri has added the Surface Cruiser, a costly but virtually indestructible pencil popper fashioned from a copolymer material. The latter ranges in sizes from the 5½-inch model, which is good for schoolies, to the 5⅞-incher (1⅞ ounces), which covers all bases, to the heavier 6⅝-inch version for casting to big bass with heavy tackle.

A fast-tip rod is preferred, and only wrist action is required to make that lure dance over the surface and spray water. Anglers often ask me what the best color is for a pencil popper, to which I simply reply that if the fish can see the color of a pencil popper you're not working it right. With large pencil poppers I prefer a long-handled spinning rod, which enables me to brace the long cork butt against my thigh and utilize an almost imperceptible wrist action to create lots of action

FISHING STRATEGIES

TROLLING large swimming plugs in areas with fish-holding structure often produces large stripers.

Swimming Plugs

Swimmers come in many sizes and shapes. The 4- to 6-inch sizes of Bombers, Rebels, Rapalas, Gag's Grabbers and Yo-Zuri Crystal Minnows, as well as other similar swimmers, are great for schoolies on light tackle and also attract some larger specimens. Many anglers rig a fly, 3- to 4-inch Felmlee eel, Fin-S-Fish or similar almost weightless lure 1½ to 2 feet ahead of the plug as a hooked teaser. This can be done with a dropper loop in the leader or by tying in a short piece of stiff leader directly to the swivel at the top of the leader. Double-headers of schoolies aren't uncommon, and some of the largest bass hit that little teaser.

Large deep-diving plugs such as the MirrOlure 113MR, Mann's Stretch 25 and Rapala Magnum can often be used on mono with success when you're seeking big bass, but most striper trophy hunters prefer large standard swimmers on wire line, as they're able to control depth accurately in that fashion.

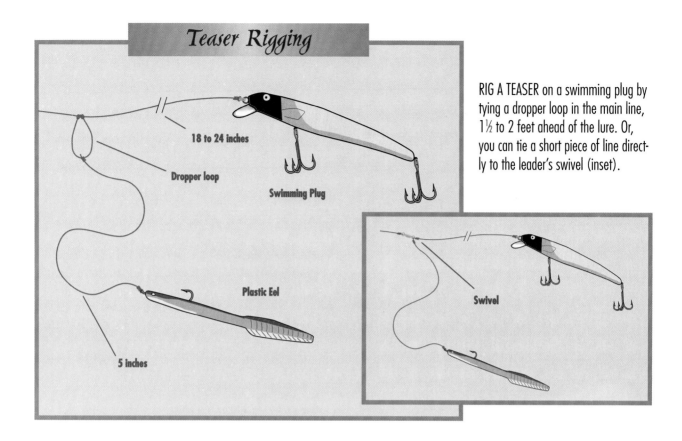

Teaser Rigging

18 to 24 inches

Dropper loop

Swimming Plug

Plastic Eel

5 inches

Swivel

RIG A TEASER on a swimming plug by tying a dropper loop in the main line, 1½ to 2 feet ahead of the lure. Or, you can tie a short piece of line directly to the leader's swivel (inset).

Several of my 50-pound bass have hit fat, 8-inch orginal wooden Danny plugs (now being produced by Gibbs). Indeed, that seems to be the problem with all wooden plugs. Many fine ones have been made over the years, but the cost of making lures out of wood is great (Stan Gibbs counted over 40 steps in the manufacture of each of his plugs). Once marketing expenses are added, wooden plugs turn out to be very expensive, and their creators almost invariably quit after a few years.

Two 50s were caught one night while I trolled Shagwong Reef at Montauk during the beginning of a mid-November snowstorm, though those were the only two bass I hooked that tide. While large plugs seem to elicit strong strikes, virtually all the bass I caught during years of fall night trolling on Shagwong Reef were hooked just barely in the jaw or on the outside of the mouth or head. Since their stomach contents consisted entirely of small young-of-the-year fish such as weakfish, sea robins, blowfish and snapper blues, I suspect that the plug may be regarded as a rival to be pushed out of the striper's feeding zone.

Large plugs are favored in most areas, but 6-inch models seem to work best in Sandy

Hook Rip. Color is a constant source of debate. I've done well with every color and feel the plug's action is most critical. Some plugs look fine but just don't swim quite right, even after the eye is bent a bit one way or the other. Black is often favored on dark nights, and Sandy Hook pro Gene Graman swears by pumpkin when baby sea robins are the prominent bait.

It's important to set the hook by continuing to move ahead with the boat while striking. Some fishermen maintain steerage and wrestle the bass back. On the other hand, if the rip isn't too high I go into neutral and drift back after solidly hooking up. Lots of wire is gained quickly in that fashion, and I'm soon right over the bass, hopefully before it straightens out the plug's treble hooks, which are heavy but vulnerable on the non-stretching wire when a big bass twists and pulls. It's essential during that manuever that the angler reel very fast in order to maintain contact with the fish and prevent slack wire from getting caught in any kelp and rocks. When the rip is too high, it's necessary to stem the current while working the bass back to the boat and hope everything holds together.

Umbrella Rigs

A unique and unusual striper lure is the umbrella, which was developed in the 1960s by Capt. Gus Pitts specifically to fool summering Montauk school stripers. He had seen relatives in Nova Scotia use lures fashioned from strips of soda cans and run from a bar to create the illusion of a school of bait. These lures fooled pollock, and Pitts figured he could do the same thing with fussy bass. What he came up with was a three-armed rig tediously fashioned by twisting heavy #15 leader wire around a drail in the middle. Codfish tubes were used as lures from leaders at the end of each arm, and smaller hookless tubes were incorporated as teasers midway along each arm.

The rig was so successful that Pitts kept it a secret until he snagged one on a party boat anchor line and the cat was out of the bag. He sold the concept to Garcia Corp. in 1969, and that company eventually produced a folding three-arm version called the Whirling Dervish. As director of field festing for Garcia at the time, I tested the Pitts Rig from my Mako 19 at Monomoy during the fall of 1969 and enjoyed the most incredible striper action—with a lure no Cape Cod striper had ever seen! Despite fishing an area I was hardly familiar with, the first day's score was 68 bass from schoolies to 34¼ pounds plus three 14- to 15-pound bluefish. The second day produced mostly larger bass, 40 up to 54 pounds, while a local pro using the standard lure at that time (a Hoochy Troll) caught only one fish!

Montauk charter skipper John Sekora soon made a rig that was more practical from a manufacturing viewpoint. It was a four-arm rig with two solid bars and four leadered tubes off the ends plus teaser tubes along each arm. This basic concept continues to this day under the banner of Sekora Lures, which are now produced by Charlie Gavin in Hicksville, Long Island.

A variation was soon created in the Metropolitan New York/New Jersey area and dubbed the Gorilla Rig by Capt. Vic Galgano, who manufactured it for years when he owned Spider Lures. The Gorilla Rig consisted of two to six take-apart heavy arms from which the tubes were directly suspended while a larger lure was run down the middle on a long leader. That rig continues today as a four-arm, one-piece model made by Julian's Tackle in Atlantic Highlands, New Jersey.

An even more unusual variation that I haven't seen in recent years was designed on Cape Cod by Freddy Bennett and proved incredibly effective from Monomoy to Nauset during the fall of 1970. It was a very short rig loaded with tubes close together right on the wire, while those at each corner also had a spinner in front. The rig was literally dragged along the bottom in 20- to 30-foot depths on only 50 to 60 feet of wire. It soon loaded up with the fine weed that was in the water that fall, though bass still hit it in that condition. The last day I dragged one off Nauset that fall produced stripers of 42½ and 55½ pounds.

Multiple catches are common with umbrellas, but it's the ability to duplicate a school of bait that is the key to their success. Tubes are still the most common lure on umbrellas, especially when sand eels are the dominant forage fish, though small spoons are often good and the latest craze is to use Sassy Shads or other soft plastics. Most pros add a much longer tube or other large lure on a long leader down the middle. Color is as much an arguing point here as with other lures, though I've never noticed much difference. White, green and red are the usual choices in tube colors.

Umbrellas are daytime lures fished almost exclusively on wire line. (See chapter entitled "Wire-Lining for Stripers" for details on using wire line.) Many anglers feel it's important to use relatively light leaders such as 40-pound when stripers are the quarry, but I never use less than 50- or 60-pound and doubt if it makes much difference. Heavier leaders untangle easier and aren't as likely to break when two large bass are pulling in opposite directions. Umbrella rigs often tangle badly when lifted aboard, so it's a good idea to have another ready to fire over while you straighten out the

first. If the bass are small enough to lift, grab the rig at the weight in the middle and simply swing it aboard in a single motion.

Spoons

A wide variety of large spoons will prove attractive to stripers, especially when fished on wire line. However, the only spoon specifically designed with jumbo stripers in mind is the bunker spoon. Originally fashioned from the chrome of car headlights, these big lures are now turned out professionally and used almost exclusively by many pros during the fall migration, when they don't want to bother with smaller bass while trying to grind out a trophy. Lots of 50- and 60-pound bass have fallen to bunker spoons, but just as many have been lost, as the heavy lure makes hooking difficult and gives the bass leverage with which to shake it.

The standard bunker spoon is chrome or stainless with a weighted keel on the back and a very large long-shanked hook attached by a screw. Most anglers add a large treble on a swivel to the bend of the hook in order to get better hook-ups. Joe Julian of Julian's Tackle in Atlantic Highlands, New Jersey, has a variation in his Montauk Bunker Spoon which features a single Siwash hook swinging at the rear on a split ring. This allows bass to twist without getting a purchase on the spoon and tearing free. White and green are other popular bunker spoon colors, and these lures are now made in several sizes.

The unique nature of the bunker spoon requires special equipment with which to work it. Bunker spoon rods are long and flexible, which not only allows the giant spoon to work correctly but transmits the throbbing of the lure to the bent rod tip so the skipper can determine at a glance if the action is proper. Since bunker spoons work best with the rod tip close to the water instead of pointing to the sky in a rod holder, side-riggers should be inserted in the holders so the rods are pointed outward from the boat.

Most bunker spoon rods have been fashioned from surf rod blanks in tackle shops and are quite expensive. Unfortunately, while working the spoon correctly, those long, heavy rods also wear out the angler just reeling in the lure, and they're torture when hooked up, as the mechanical advantage favors the fish. However, Seeker Rod. Co. has developed 8- and 9-foot (BA1153M) one-piece models that are much lighter and easier on the angler while still doing the most important job of working the spoon.

Trolling speed for bunker spoons must be just right in order to get the proper action, and it's often difficult to fish other types of lures when using them. The wide sweep of spoons from side to side makes it even more important that both wires be of equal length and set as far apart as possible. Care must be taken in making turns, particularly over rough bottom, as the combined weight of the spoon, wire line and any drail added to the rig will plunge to bottom with any slack.

Bunker spoons may provoke strikes from bass even when there are plenty of bunker for the taking in the same area. Bunkers were so thick one autumn in Sandy Hook Bay that we were constantly snagging them with spoons trolled from Gene Graman's skiff, *That's It.* It seemed ridiculous to try fooling a striper into hitting a big piece of metal when there were thousands of seemingly helpless and tightly packed bunkers on the surface and many more below them. But we did hook bass, and most of them had nothing in their stomachs despite the easy pickings all around.

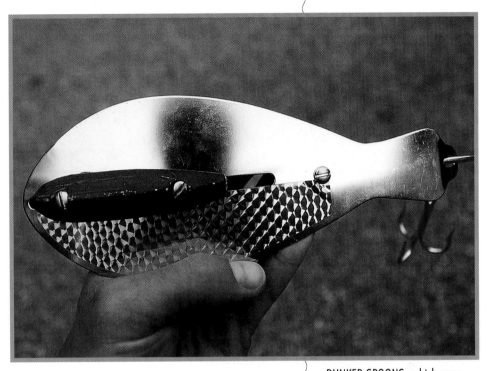

BUNKER SPOONS, which were designed with jumbo bass in mind, work best when trolled on wire line.

Whereas most other lures are trolled over structure or where bass are obviously feeding, bunker spoons can be utilized with some success while trolling blind over sand or mud bottoms for stray large stripers. It isn't even necessary to get them near bottom, as the noise and flash of the spoon will attract bass from some distance.

In addition to the unique bunker spoon, there are a number of more standard-type large spoons which often work as well or even better at times. Colors other than the usual chrome or white are catching on, with green being a particular favorite when herring or mackerel need to be imitated rather than bunkers. The use of stick-on tapes to create additional flash and a personalized presentation is also become more common.

Spoons are great line twisters, and anglers using them must be careful to use quality heavy-duty swivels. Some pros rig a second swivel in the middle of a long leader in order to cut down on that problem.

Metal Casting Lures

These lures go way back in striper fishing history. As a group they used to be called "tin squids," and the act of casting them was referred to as squidding—though those terms are rarely heard any longer. Tin was the most popular material for making such lures in the 1930s and 1940s, and many of the craftsmen (such as Charlie Pasquale) who fashioned block tin squids in many variations became famous. Tin was an ideal material in that it was supple enough to shape and could be buffed up to provide a unique, soft shine.

SQUIDDING, or casting metal lures, will catch fish from the bottom to the surface.

Hopkins changed the direction of the metal lure business with the use of stainless steel, which was expensive and difficult to work with. Many less costly chrome-plated metals were also developed and proved very effective. The Acme Kastmaster, Luhr Jensen Krocodile, Hopkins NO=EQL and others have also risen to the top of the list in many striper anglers' tackle boxes, as all have slightly different actions and casting properties. Since bass are usually feeding on some sort of shiny forage, metal lures are a natural for casting and also provide versatility, since they can be worked deep as well as on or near the surface simply by altering the drop rate after casting and by the subsequent retrieve ratio. Additional action can also be easily imparted by tip movement or even varying the retrieve.

Thus, the same lure that is often effective when being reeled fast right on the surface can also take the place of the diamond jig by being bounced or retrieved off bottom. A variety of sizes should be available in order to match both the equipment used, the size of the forage and the portion of the water column to be worked. For instance, though a greedy striper feeding on the surface might hit a 3-ounce Hopkins as well as a 1-ounce version, a very fast retrieve would be required to keep the heavier metal up in the water, and chances are it would have to be zipped through the feeding zone too quickly to be effective. Unlike bluefish, stripers generally prefer a slower-moving lure and will often ignore those that look like they require too much effort to catch. On the other hand, that heavy model may be required if bass are feeding deeper during a windy day and the drift prevents the lighter version from getting down to the proper depth quickly enough.

The plain metal lure continues to produce, but the concept of dressings on the hook has expanded from the feathers which were common decades ago to include bucktail, artificial hair, tubes and soft plastics. The dressed metal is often more effective, and while sharp-toothed bluefish will destroy the dressing or tube they'll also tend to hit at that area rather than on the metal itself—thus preventing cut-offs.

Profile is frequently an important factor and should be kept in mind when deciding whether to use metal plain or with dressing, since the latter presents a longer shape that may or may not reflect the length of the bait stripers are feeding on. Another factor to consider is that bulky dressings such as tubes and plastics will inhibit casts into the wind, and if distance is a consideration it might be best to use the plain metal lure.

Whether with or without dressing, I prefer single hook metals to the old standard trebles. In my experience, single hooks seem to provide similar hook-up rates, and bass don't seem to twist off them as readily as on trebles. Most importantly, the single is easier and safer to remove, and in this era when the vast majority of stripers are being released, the single hook does the least amount of damage to the fish.

As with all casting lures, I rig by tying a short double line with a Bimini Twist before using an Albright knot to add a piece of leader mono or fluorocarbon material. That leader should be long enough that you can reach over the side to grab it and haul smaller fish aboard for release—but just short enough so the knot clears your tiptop for easy casting. I don't consider leader size to be critical with lures which are retrieved at a relatively rapid rate, but since striper teeth are too small to be of great concern, 30-pound is sufficient for schoolies and 40- to 50-pound works well for larger bass.

Heavy-duty snaps make lure changes easy, and knots can be difficult to draw tight on metal lures that don't have a split ring to tie to. However, I'm always leery about having anything in my terminal rigging that could be opened up by a twisting fish or left open by the angler in the excitement of getting a lure out to feeding bass. As with swimming plugs, the addition of an almost weightless lure (called a teaser even though it carries a hook) ahead of a metal can greatly increase your chances of success under some circumstances and can also lead to some double-headers. However, if one of those bass is large it may well be lost if something gives during the tug-o-war. Swivels aren't necessary with casting metal, though one can be used instead of a dropper loop in the leader to tie in the teaser.

Bluefish, with their sharp teeth, present a special challenge for striper anglers. Teasers aren't a good idea when blues are numerous unless you don't mind frequent cut-offs. I also go to heavier leaders when the two species are mixed since stripers aren't too line-shy when in competition for food with choppers. Whereas heavy mono won't hurt your lure presentation much, wire is a no-no, as it changes lure action so much that I've even seen blues refuse to hit.

DIAMOND JIGS are particularly effective when bass are holding near bottom in deep water.

Diamond Jigs

There's not a great deal of difference between these metal lures and those designed primarily for casting, except that their shape provides a better sink rate while providing little inherent action. Most of these jigs don't have the old diamond shape popular for cod, but come in many slim variations that have the common goal of sinking rapidly and staying close to bottom.

Older diamond jigs were equipped either with a treble hook at the end or a built-in single hook. It wasn't until Artie Frey came up with a better mousetrap in the form of his Ava jig with a swivel and a single hook on the business end that the diamond jig really caught on. That jig eliminated the "purchase" that fish previously used to twist off, and is also far less harmful to those that are to be released. That version of the diamond is now so universal in the Northeast that it's usually referred to as an "Ava" even though that company went out of business many years ago. The size designations used by Ava also tend to be utilized by other small manufacturers,

BEGIN WORKING a diamond jig by free-falling it to the bottom (white-dashed line). Apply just enough thumb pressure to keep the reel from backlashing. Just as the jig hits the bottom, reel up two or three fast turns (orange-dashed line). Then pause for a moment (yellow dot). Reel up another two or three turns. Repeat until you are approximatly 10 turns above the bottom, then repeat the process.

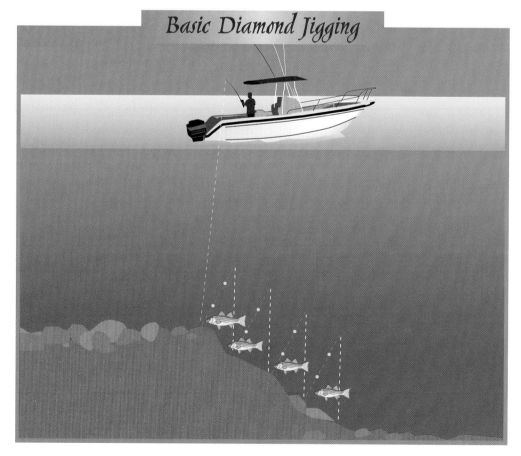

Basic Diamond Jigging

with the 27 being a 3-ounce model and an 007 being the little 1-ounce version.

Diamond jigs have little inherent action, and that's just the way stripers usually prefer them. This is especially true when sand eels are the dominant forage, since those slim baitfish rise lazily out of the bottom and a diamond jig being retrieved slowly seems to resemble them. Bluefish prefer a fast retrieve almost to the surface and with some added action. On the other hand, bass and weakfish are most often fooled with a slow retrieve only about halfway to the surface.

It's almost too simple to be effective, but my usual method of working a diamond jig involves a free-fall to bottom with no thumbing except to prevent a backlash—though it's important to be ready to immediately go into gear and reel tight if a bump is felt on the way down. As soon as the jig hits, the reel is engaged, and two or three fast turns are used to bounce it off bottom before the retrieve is slowed. Unless there's reason to think bass are much higher in the water column, I only come up 10 turns or so before pausing an instant and then repeating the free-fall.

Hits most often occur on the pause or the drop, and the angler must be ready to respond instantly. Don't expect solid smashes, as what you'll get most often is only a bump. Go into gear at any such sign and reel tight to the fish rather than strike against what might be slack line.

Jigs work best in a vertical plane and seem to be much less effective as the angle increases. Keep this in mind during a fast drift, as you'll be opening that angle constantly every time you drop back. Frequent reeling up and dropping down is required under such circumstances. On calm days it may not be necessary to continuously retrieve and re-set.

On party boats you'll notice the pros stay on the downwind side and flip their jigs out so they hit bottom underneath the boat. Only two or three drop-backs may be possible before the jig has to be retrieved and flipped out again. By keeping the jig in a more vertical plane and presenting it to the fish first, those pros almost always catch more than the fishermen comfortably jigging on the upwind side

Party Boat Jigging

Wind

POSITION YOURSELF on the downwind side of a party boat. Cast the jig ahead of the boat and allow it to free-fall to the bottom. Work the jig (opposite page) off the bottom, then drop it back to the bottom again. The jig will be almost directly below the boat. After two or three drop-backs, before the boat drifts over the jig, reel up, cast ahead of the boat and repeat the process.

with their lines stretched far away from the boat and probably out of the payoff zone most of the time.

While bluefish are great game fish and often the target species, when it comes to catching stripers in a mixed fishery the choppers are just a big pain in the neck. Since they prefer faster-moving lures and tend to populate higher levels of the water column, slower jigging will reduce bluefish hits and leave your jig available to a striper while other anglers are spending all their time fighting and removing blues from their jigs.

A trip to Manasquan Ridge, New Jersey, during a cold, windy day in November emphasized that point. There were so many migrating bluefish, they could literally be hooked on every drop, but I soon tired of that and started concentrating on the bottom. By ignoring taps on the way down and working the jig slowly within a few feet of bottom, I caught almost every striper hooked that day and cut down on the volume of blues while my friends hooked hardly anything but choppers and lost lots of jigs in the process.

There are times when stripers are higher in the water column, and diamonds should be retrieved further or even worked on the sur-

In addition to the plain diamond jig, there's an even more common version with a tube tail. That tube, rigged over a long bent hook to give it action, was designed with bluefish in mind and is perfect for that species, since they tend to chop baitfish from the rear, and in doing so with the tube they're far away from the jig and a potential cut-off. The tube also increases the all-important profile of the lure, which is good if the bait is long but is not the ticket for more discriminating stripers when they're on short bait. As a result, I most often stick with plain diamonds for bass, though I've also done very well with tubes.

Diamond jigging is most frequently done blind, though working birds and breaking fish provide clues in the fall. Therefore, it's basically a technique to be used over structure such as rips and underwater hills. Simply run uptide ahead of the structure, allowing enough time to get the jigs to bottom before entering the payoff zone, and drift through until well past the drop on the other side. Though I generally don't believe that light leaders are a must for jigging bass, there was a time decades ago in the Montauk rips when the pros scoring most heavily were tying directly to 12-pound mono.

DIAMOND JIG
with tube tail

face. Though their shape works against them as a surface lure, diamonds can be utilized in that fashion by going to lighter weights and somewhat faster retrieves. However, even when stripers are showing on the surface there are usually many more and possibly bigger specimens below—a possibility which should not be ignored.

Another method of working a rip with a jig involves stemming the current. Position your boat uptide of the rip and apply just enough speed to hold position while the anglers drop jigs back. The strong current will sweep your jig back in a flash. As soon as the jig hits bottom, reel a couple of turns, pause, and drop back again. During a strong current

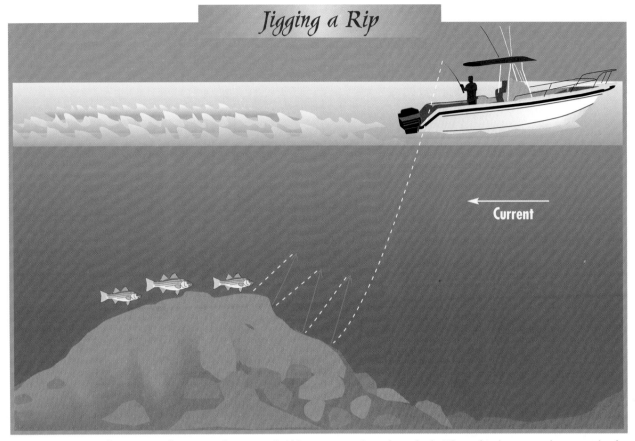

STEM THE CURRENT above a rip with just enough power to hold boat position. Drop the jig back. When it hits bottom, reel up a couple of turns, pause, then drop it back again. Reel up and repeat.

you'll only get two to three drops before having to reel in and start all over. It's a lot of work, but very effective when done correctly. Light lines cut through the water best, and 4- to 6-ounce jigs are most often used during the middle of the current before you can drop down to 3-ounce models toward the slack. The same braided wire lines now being used for bunker chunking may well prove effective for this method.

The standard chrome color seems to be used by just about every diamond-jigger, though gold jigs also work. There was also a period years ago when Montauk jiggers used diamonds with coverings of yellow, red and other colors, which all seemed to have their moments.

Leadheads & Other Jigs

This very broad category includes all the many lures which employ a lead or other metal head for weight to which dressings of various types are attached for casting, jigging or trolling.

The traditional bucktail jig has long been one of the most effective of all school striper lures, whether cast in protected bays and rivers or in near-shore ocean and sound waters. It imitates most small, slim baitfish such as spearing and anchovies, and is easy to cast and work with light tackle. I assumed it had been around "forever" until rereading the classic book *Striped Bass* by O.H.P. Rodman (A. S. Barnes & Co., N.Y., 1944). The author writes about being amazed at watching other anglers catching bass with a strange lure as he was unsuccessfully trolling with seaworms on a spinner in the North River, in Massachusetts. The "secret" lure turned out to be a Barracuda, a small white feather jig made in Florida. Rodman had already noted that small metal-headed feather jigs—such as those with a hole for the line through the head used for school tuna—were standards for trolling stripers at that time.

LEADHEAD JIGS have long been one of the most effective lures for catching stripers.

Those tuna jigs are no longer used for stripers, but other types of jigs have become trolling standards in many areas. Bucktail jigs in 1- to 2-ounce sizes are most commonly employed, but the favorite at Montauk and on the clam beds off Barnegat Inlet, New Jersey, is the parachute jig, in which some of the artificial hair is tied backwards so the lure creates a pulsing appearance when jigged, probably resembling a squid. Regardless of the type, a piece of Uncle Josh pork rind or something similar is added to the hook for extra attraction. White is the usual pork rind color, but yellow, red and green are also popular.

Regardless of type, the key to success with jigs in daytime trolling is getting them near bottom and imparting lots of jigging action. Wire line allows the motion imparted by the fisherman to be transmitted to the lure, which may be 300 feet away, and results usually end up in proportion to the amount of effort expended. A push-pull motion with the rod is least tiring, but this is no sport for the lazy—especially when there's a lot of line out.

Since this isn't the type of fishing anglers would enjoy doing when it's just a shot in the dark, jig trolling is practiced over structure where results are likely to come quickly. Just as with trolling other types of lures in structure, jigs must be placed in front of the rip or bottom configuration and worked in the payoff zone as the skipper keeps track of depth and indicates when line has to be dropped back or taken up. More so than with other lures, jigs should be worked very close to bottom and even bounced at times. Because the hook rides up, jigs don't get snagged as much as other lures, though they will pick up kelp and other weed.

There are situations in which jigging isn't

necessary. For instance, jigs seem to work quite well at night when simply dragged just over bottom. Indeed, in the fall they probably imitate the young-of-the-year fish that stripers usually feed on much better than the large plugs we normally troll.

Another effective means of fishing a jig without jigging doesn't even involve trolling, though you'll be moving about as fast with the current. In such areas as Plum Gut on Long Island and at The Race between Long Island and Fisher's Island, jigs are drifted with a sinker rig. This is usually a simple three-way swivel set-up with a long leader to the jig and a lighter leader to the sinker, since break-offs are common in the rocky bottom. The jig is literally fished as a live bait, just as described in the bait section with eels, mackerel or bunkers. Drop it to bottom ahead of the underwater structure to be fished and then reel up a couple of turns. Keep an eye on the recorder and reel up or drop down as required, but always stay a couple of feet off bottom in order to prevent constant hangs. A special jig often used in this fishery is made with a plastic head so it floats and presumably provides better action.

Smaller leadheads, especially bucktail jigs, are among the best of all schoolie lures in the hands of an experienced angler who can impart just enough action to make the jig look like the real thing and is alert to the light bumps that are often all you'll feel in the way of a hit. In strong currents the hit may simply be a change in movement as the bass stops the jig. Just as in trolling, a slim strip of pork rind provides action to a lure lacking any except the little hops provided by the angler's rod tip. If in doubt about size, go a bit lighter than you think will be necessary. In waters with little current, a ¼-ounce jig is normally sufficient, and even in fast water you'll probably be casting uptide with only ½- to ⅝-ounce jigs. The idea is for the current to sweep them along just above bottom on the retrieve, and heavier jigs will hang up constantly.

Though small bucktail jigs are intended for schoolies, much larger stripers will inhale them at times. On one occasion I was casting bucktails and catching schoolies steadily on light spinning tackle near Montauk Lighthouse when a much bigger fish grabbed the lure. It took some time before I had that bass alongside—a 32-pounder. The little bucktail and pork rind looked ridiculous next to that fish, but chances are it would have ignored a live bunker if I had had one. Since the big bass was feeding on the same small bait as the schoolies, "matching the hatch" was just as effective for her as for the smaller stripers.

Head shapes can make a difference under various circumstances, and every serious angler has his favorite. One of the original hot bucktail jigs was the Upperman, made by two New Jersey brothers who found that a flattish or lima-bean shape provided more action in a current. One of my mentors, the late Capt. Bud Henderson, would use nothing but Smilin' Bill bucktails and pork rind while trolling bass commercially with handlines off Nantucket, Massachusetts, during the 1960s. Those jigs had a "V" in the head that also seemed to provide some action. Most jig heads are bullet-shaped or round, though there are many variations even in basic shapes such as the Potbelly. Just slide a plastic body on and see how it works. If you don't like the combination, it takes only seconds to switch to another body.

The concept of using plastics on a lead head was popularized by the late Al Reinfelder, who developed both the Alou Eel and the Bait Tail, which he and Lou Palma first made in 1960. The Bait Tail incorporated a standard jig head with the eye on top and a soft molded-plastic body on the hook designed to imitate any small baitfish. What was soft then would now be considered hard when placed alongside plastics like the Fin-S-Fish, but the concept was there and Reinfelder actually wrote a short book, *Bait Tail Fishing*, about it.

Plastics have become even more popular in recent years for use on leadhead jigs. A great variety of plastic baits can be utilized, and all work under various conditions. Kalin's, Mr. Twister, Lunker City, Mr. Wiffle, Newport, DOA and many others make an unlimited number of stlyes ranging from action tails to soft slim bodies like the Fin-S-Fish. Once again it's a matter of matching the hatch when it comes to selecting length, shape and color of the bodies to be placed on the heads.

There are many variations of the lead-head jig, some of which don't even look much

LEADHEAD JIGS are available in many sizes, shapes and colors and with many types of dressings. They are effective whether you prefer to cast, troll or drift.

like the basic lure. For instance, the Hoochy Troll, which was developed by Weber Tackle for bluefish, turned out to be a great striper lure in Pleasant Bay on Cape Cod during the 1960s, when squid flooded in during the spring. The lead head of the Hoochy Troll was inside the colorful skirts, and a chain was attached leading to a single hook. Trolled on lead-core line in the bay's shallow channels, bright red Hoochys were unbeatable until the squid runs disappeared.

Artificial Eels

The Alou Eel was a big hit among striper fishermen for both casting and trolling during the 1960s, before bluefish became abundant and the cost of losing plastic bodies became too great for most anglers, who switched to more durable lures. However, the effectiveness of plastic eels rigged on lead squid heads has never diminished, especially for night fishing. The smallest sizes of those

TUBE LURES have become standard for taking trophy striped bass. Some anglers tip their tubes with a piece of sandworm for added attraction.

lures are also effective when large sand eels are the dominant bait.

Tube Lures

In addition to the smaller tubes used on umbrella rigs, long tube lures have become standards over the years for wire line trolling. These lures were developed during the post-World War II years. I was introduced to them in the early 1960s by a Manhattan pro named Vince Scotti, a gentleman from the old school who wore a coat and tie under slickers in his skiff while trolling New York Bight and Sandy Hook waters for big stripers. Scotti created his tubes from surgical tubing, which was dyed to various colors and heated in his oven just enough to create the desired shape, then rigged through with heavy mono to a hook several inches behind the head and to another at the rear. Setting those hooks just right so the 15- to 18-inch tubes would swim correctly was vital.

SMALL PLUGS used on light tackle are very effective on bass in shallow bays near the surf line.

Scotti used no weight at the head, and it was difficult to get tension on the almost weightless tube when sending it astern, but the results were excellent both in his local waters and when I later started using tubes at Montauk. Many anglers still make their own tubes, but there are also commercial models available from such firms as Sekora Lures that work very well either as a single lure or as a larger lure, usually run back on a long leader from the middle of an umbrella rig.

Some tubes are made with a lead at the head for weight, such as the largest of them all—the Sekora Striper Viper, which is 30 inches long and fitted with four single hooks. Other tubes are fitted to a lead action head. However, I prefer the weightless tube, which best resembles an eel and can be worked easily on wire close to bottom without hanging up. With such tubes it's best to troll as slow as you can, just barely more than stemming the current. As with a plug, move the rod tip forward every so often to ensure that the action is there and the tube is free of any weed.

Tubes are effective both night and day, but be sure to use a swivel ahead of the leader to prevent twisting. Color is a matter of preference, which changes by area and often year by year. Natural tubing has always been a favorite, while black, white, red, green and purple are other effective choices.

A variation is the much longer, rather stiff semi-circular tube tipped with a piece of sandworm and dragged along bottom on wire line by southern New England anglers. That odd technique has been used with great success, especially during the dog days of summer, when stripers tend to be lazy, by anglers in eastern Connecticut and Rhode Island for many years but hasn't spread to other areas.

Small Plugs

Just about any small plug, even fresh water models, will work for stripers at times, as inland anglers have learned while fishing in the many lakes, impoundments and rivers throughout the country where striped bass have been introduced. Small swimming plugs and poppers have already been discussed, but light-tackle anglers shouldn't overlook darters and such specialized models as the lipless MirrOlure 52M which is especially effective in shallow bay waters and when young-of-the-year mullet are migrating south near the surf line. Action must be imparted to the MirrOlure by erratic jerks of the rod tip to make it appear to be an injured fish.

—*Al Ristori*

FISHING STRATEGIES

WIRE-LINING FOR STRIPERS

Striped bass are fundamentally lazy creatures. If given the choice they prefer to have their meals delivered rather than having to chase them down. That's why stripers seek out areas of strong current, especially those spots where they can hide behind a ledge, boulder or other piece of bottom structure and ambush baitfish caught in the flow. Furthermore, most stripers, especially the biggest fish, are loathe to stray very far to grab a passing morsel. To catch these fish you've got to make it easy for them, and that means getting your lures down to their level. There are several ways to do this, but wire line is one of the easiest and most effective.

Selecting Rods & Reels

While some fishermen use different wire-line outfits depending on the size of the fish they're targeting and the type of lures they're fishing, a good all-round system begins with a rod rated for 40- or 50-pound-test and a conventional (revolving spool) 4/0 reel. For fishing parachute jigs, a standard wire-line lure, Capt. Bob DeCosta of Nantucket, Massachusetts, recommends a 6- to 6½-foot, medium-taper rod with a stiff tip. (After you get more proficient at wire-lining, you may want a more flexible tip to give the lures more action.)

Whether you go with a custom-built stick or a production model (many tackle companies, such as Penn, offer rods designed specifically for wire-line fishing), the rod must feature carbide or titanium guides to withstand the constant rubbing of the wire. Ideally, the tiptop should be an oversized roller model to help prevent the wire from kinking and allow the bulky knots to pass through. However, many experts get by just fine with oversized ring tiptops. AFTCO makes a series of special guides designed for wire, all featuring a heavy-duty finish.

Popular reels for wire-lining include the Daiwa 400H Sealine, the Penn 113H Senator and the Shimano TLD 20. Those with high-speed gear ratios come in handy for making quick depth adjustments over rapidly changing bottom.

Most full-service tackle stores can set you up with the necessary backing and wire, but here are some basic guidelines if you want to do it yourself. Start with 150 to 200 feet of 100- to 130-pound-test

Stripers seek out strong-current areas near bottom structure to ambush baitfish. To catch these bass you must get your lures down to their level.

FISHING STRATEGIES

83

Dacron backing (some anglers prefer monofilament backing). DeCosta starts with 100 feet of 70-pound Dacron, which he splices to a 70-foot section of 130-pound Dacron. The idea is that the heavier Dacron will better stand up to being rubbed across the guides. This is particularly important when trolling jigs, since the rod is often pumped to provide more action, causing the same section of line to be rubbed across the guide surface repeatedly. Even though Dacron is tough stuff, you should check it often for frays.

To attach the Dacron backing to the wire, DeCosta splices a loop in the Dacron, then folds it over and runs the wire through the loop. Then he makes a small, tight loop in the wire with a haywire twist. The resulting connection is similar to the interlocking loop-to-loop system used in fly fishing and makes it impossible for the wire to cut into the Dacron. DeCosta advises making a short haywire twist (seven or eight turns) to prevent kinking.

How Much Wire?

The amount of wire you'll need depends largely on water depth. As a basic rule, you can figure on ten feet of wire for every foot of depth. This amount will vary depending on current speed, lure weight, wind, and boat speed, but you can always achieve more depth by letting out more backing or switching to a heavier lure.

Rhode Island charter captain Mitch Chagnon, who fishes from Long Island to Narragansett Bay, says that in a moderate current he'll use 300 feet of wire to get a two-ounce jig near the bottom in 30 feet of water. As the current picks up, he'll switch to a heavier jig, sometimes using as much as 10 ounces during peak tidal flow. Chagnon uses two 150-foot sections of 60-pound wire on his basic wire-line rig. These are separated by a 15-foot "bridge" of heavy Dacron. If he wants to fish shallower, he can let out 150 feet and still have the protection of the Dacron.

DeCosta, who fishes primarily over shoals in 15 to 30 feet of water, uses 150 feet of wire on his reels. With all the wire out and a four-ounce jig, he figures the line will be down 20 to 22 feet in a moderate current. If the fish are deeper or if he needs to account for a stronger current, he'll simply let out more backing or switch to a heavier jig.

Massachusetts charter captain Bill Reynolds, who fishes the many ledges, rocks and shoals around Buzzards Bay, Martha's Vineyard and the Elizabeth Islands, spools up with 125 feet of wire and also adjusts his depth by letting out more backing. To make things easier for his charter clients, he marks his backing in 10-foot increments with black twine. A single black marker is used for 10 feet, two black markers are used for 20 feet, and three for 30. This makes it easy for his anglers to adjust the depth of their lures, since Reynolds can tell them which marker to let out past the rod tip as he monitors his depth-sounder. In 25 feet of water and with a moderate current running, Reynolds lets out 125 feet of wire and 20 feet of backing to place a four-ounce jig a foot or two above the bottom. Letting out line to the third mark (30 feet of backing) will get the lure down to about 30 feet in the same conditions.

Leaders tend to be long in wire-lining, since the bass can be spooky at times. Reynolds uses a 10-foot leader, while DeCosta prefers 15 to 20 feet. Both captains use monofilament and attach the leader to the wire via an Albright knot (opposite page), although you can also make the connection with a swivel. Most experts prefer knots to swivels, however, since swivels can jam in the roller tip and are more visible to the fish. They are also more likely to snag weeds.

DeCosta's heaviest leaders are 80-pound mono, but he'll scale down to 30-pound if the water's very clear and the fish are acting shy. Since Reynolds often fishes around rocky ledges and boulders, he prefers 100-pound test to protect against abrasion. "Sometimes you have to bounce the line right on the bottom, and after a while that 100-pound leader may wear down to 50," he says. Also, he doesn't want to take any chances in case he hooks a monster fish. "You've got to be ready for that 50- or 60-pounder, and you can't beat a fish like that with 20- or 30-pound leader."

Another reason for using heavy leaders is bluefish, which often feed alongside the bass and can make for an expensive trip if they continuously cut you off. The best advice is to

Albright Knot

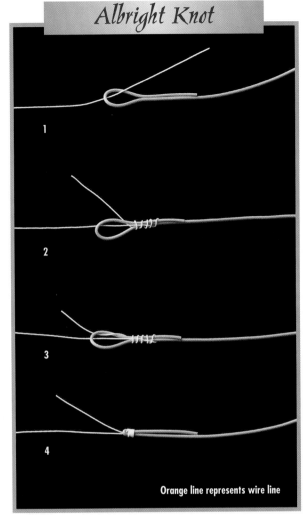

Orange line represents wire line

DOUBLE UP (1) last 2 inches of wire line and pass tag end of backing or leader through loop. (2) Wind backing or leader over itself and doubled line five to eight times, depending on line diameter. (3) Pass backing or leader through loop so it comes out on the same side it entered. (4) Tighten by slowly pulling on all four lines. Pull until knot is tight; trim ends closely.

start out with a heavy leader. If you can see fish on your depthsounder but they're not biting, keep scaling down in leader size until you start getting hits.

Speaking of depthsounders, a good one is an invaluable tool in wire-lining, especially if you've never fished a particular area before. Experts like Chagnon say to "get the best one you can afford," since you need to know what the bottom structure looks like, the precise depth of the water and the depth at which the fish are holding. In fact, Reynolds often targets individual fish by adjusting his lure depth according to the marks on his screen.

Where to Fish Wire

Now that you know what equipment you'll need for wire-line fishing, let's look at where to fish. Most anglers use wire to fish rips, where strong currents keep the biggest fish holding close to the bottom. Rips are usually formed by changes in depth, such as where a ledge, reef or sandbar rises towards the surface. This sudden narrowing of the water column causes the current to flow faster, creating a line of choppy water or large waves along the downcurrent edge of the structure. This distinct edge of rough water is known as the "rip line."

The tricky thing about rips is that they can be very long, with the fish often moving to different points along the rip as the current changes. Rip masters like DeCosta, Chagnon and Reynolds know from years of experience exactly where the fish will be at different stages of the tide. Newcomers, on the other hand, have to put in their time before they can expect to score consistently.

To learn a rip, you've got to take a systematic approach. Once you hook a fish, take a land bearing or hit the event marker on your GPS. Note also your exact position, the exact stage of the tide, wind direction, time of day and other variables. When these conditions occur again, chances are that the fish will be in the exact same spot.

Obviously, a depthsounder can be used to locate fish along a rip, but there are other ways to find them. One is to look for birds such as gannets and terns working along a particular section of the rip. Another is to find a sharp bend or point in the rip line, which often indicates a place where baitfish have become concentrated. A third way to locate the bass is to move laterally along the rip line until you get a strike or start marking fish on your sounder. Chagnon often does this when the current is weak, since the bass tend to spread out and more boat speed is needed to keep the lures swimming properly.

While stripers will generally move to the section of a rip with the most current, Chagnon warns that this isn't always so. "Sometimes the current will be so strong that the bass aren't fast enough to grab the bait that's passing by overhead," he says. "In this case, they may move to a spot where there's less current, even if there isn't as much bait around."

Chagnon advises working another section of the rip after making four or five passes over one spot without a strike. If you see fish on your sounder, don't give up—but don't pound them either, he adds. Instead, give them a rest and return a little later. Keep working the fish with different lures and approaches and eventually you'll find the key to making them strike.

How to Fish a Rip

As you might have gathered, skillful boat-handling is the real key to wire-line fishing. Be extremely cautious when approaching a rip, especially a big open-ocean rip with steep

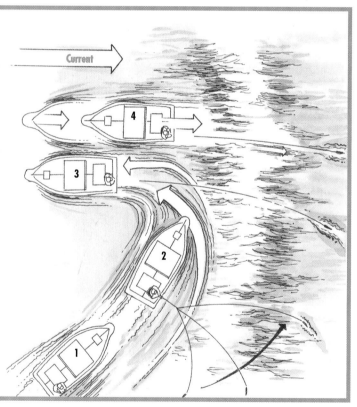

FISH A RIP with wire line by approaching from the side, angling slightly downcurrent (1). As the boat nears the rip, swing the bow directly upcurrent and stem the tide, allowing the lures to swing in behind the shoal (2). When the lines begin to straighten behind the boat, throttle forward to bring the lures over the shoal (3). Work the lures over the shoal (4) by easing back towards the rip and then slowly throttling forward.

standing waves. If you fail to make your turn upcurrent in time, you could get caught broadside in the rip and broach.

The best way to approach a rip is at an angle, with the bow facing slightly downcurrent. As the boat approaches the rip, the helmsman should swing the bow upcurrent and stem the tide using the boat's power. DeCosta calls this a slip turn, and it allows the lures to swing in behind the shoal to where the stripers are holding. When the lines have straightened behind the boat, the helmsman should throttle forward, pulling the lures over the shoal, then throttle back to let the lures sweep back through the rip again. The lines can also be worked parallel to the rip by angling the bow slightly into the current and using just enough power to maintain position ahead of the rip. When searching for fish, be sure to work both sides of the rip, since stripers may hold in front of the structure, directly on top of the structure or some distance downcurrent.

Wire line can also be fished effectively around large individual boulders, riprap islands, bridge pilings, wrecks and other large objects. For example, Reynolds likes to fish a series of sunken barge containers in Buzzards Bay. The bass like to hold on the downcurrent side of the rectangular metal containers, waiting to ambush prey, and Reynolds catches them by pulling his lures tight to the edge of the structure.

Beaches and banks offer many opportunities for using wire. Along many beaches, such as those along western Rhode Island, Long Island, and Cape Cod, wave action and swift currents running parallel to shore can scoop out deep pockets and troughs on the bottom, perfect spots for striped bass to ambush baitfish. In this case, the lines should be pulled parallel to the shore, with the anglers letting out more line as the lures pass over the bottom depressions.

Parachutes and Tubes

Perhaps the most popular and effective lure in wire-line fishing is the parachute jig, which is designed to imitate squid and large baitfish. Parachutes come in different weights, making them ideal for fishing different depths with a single length of wire. White and chartreuse seem to be the best colors, probably because they're more visible in deep or off-colored water. Most charter captains agree that the addition of a long pork-rind strip really increases the effectiveness of these jigs.

Parachute jigs can be fished without the angler imparting any action at all, but most pros like to pump the rod tip to make the lure look like a squid pulsing through the water. Some anglers find it easier to jig with the rod inverted, holding it like they would a broom with the tip next to the water. This also puts the jigs closer to the bottom.

Reynolds like to fish jigs early in the season but switches to long tube lures as the summer wears on. A tube lure is a long (20-36 inches) section of curved rubber tubing with a single hook on the end and an egg sinker stuffed in the front for weight. To add scent appeal, a large seaworm is usually placed on the hook. White, red, and black are good tube colors.

Tubes need not be jigged to be effective; indeed, many captains simply leave the rod in a gunwale holder. However, in order for a tube to be most effective, there needs to be a slight bend in the wire that runs through the lure. The ideal action is a slow, lazy roll that looks like a swimming eel. Before letting out your tubes, troll them next to the boat to make sure they're swimming properly.

Umbrellas, Plugs and Spoons

Umbrella rigs are very effective when fished on wire, especially in areas where small baitfish, such as sand eels or silversides, are present. A large plug rigged to swim behind the tubes sometimes turns the trick with finicky bass. Many captains feel that the plug imitates a pursuing predator, thereby triggering the striper's competitive feeding instinct.

Large swimming plugs like the Gibbs Danny or Rapala Magnum also work well when fished by themselves on wire. Just remember that these plugs will dive even deeper after being let out, so watch your depth. A swimming plug outfitted with an eel-skin can also be effective, especially at night. And speaking of eels, live ones can also be fished on wire—just be sure to troll them slow.

Metal spoons like the Tony Acetta Pet, the Huntington Drone, and the Clark Spoon are effective when medium-sized herring, menhaden and mackerel are abundant. When large herring or menhaden (bunker, pogies) are in the area, the Reliable Bunker Spoon is a great lure to troll on wire. This large, metal lure should be fished very slowly to make it flash and roll like an injured bait. It's a great lure for really big bass.

Fighting Fish on Wire

If you've never fished wire line before, the strike of a fish, especially a big fish, will probably surprise you. Because wire doesn't stretch like monofilament, which can act as a kind of shock-absorber, the impact of the strike is transferred immediately to the rod. Once the fight begins, you can feel every head shake, even with 300 feet of wire between you and the fish.

Because of its lack of stretch, wire line requires a gentle touch on the part of the angler, especially if the fish is hooked in strong current; otherwise the hooks can easily be pulled from the fish's soft mouth. Always make sure the drag is set properly at the beginning of each trip, and never try to horse the fish in. Use gentle pumps of the rod to work the fish to the boat, and always wait for the fish to finish a run before attempting to gain line.

In a rip-fishing situation, it's the helmsman's job to keep the boat stationary while the fish is being fought. If a fish refuses to budge from the rip, pulling on it from different angles sometimes works. As a last resort, and only if it is safe to do so, let the boat drift through the rip and pull on the fish from the downcurrent side.

On a final note, pay special attention to maintenance of your wire-line outfit. Always wash your equipment thoroughly with soap and fresh water, and give the wire a gently misting of WD-40 after each use. Also, check the wire for kinks and the backing for nicks and frays. If you fish with wire frequently, it's a good idea to replace the line after each season. It's a simple thing to do, and it could make the difference between the catch of a lifetime and the one that got away.

—*Tom Richardson*

SHORE FISHING FOR STRIPED BASS

Perhaps the effort and expense are realized at dusk when the sun sinks below layers of ominous clouds and the rod bends double with the jolting strike of a trophy bass.

FISHING STRATEGIES

At some early point in one's shore-fishing career, after a few wrong turns and trials followed by error, there's a decision made to continue with the sport, to overlook the mistakes and instead savor the glorious sunrises or watch the moon step up over glistening white water and anticipate the action in the night ahead.

As you move forward with your new "career," you'll likely acquire more gear, catch more and perhaps larger stripers, learn the sport in-depth, then turn to watch as others trace the footsteps you've taken to a great life of catching striped bass from the "shingle," the world of the surfcaster.

Choosing Rods and Reels

Nothing makes the surfman's (or surfwoman's) lot easier than good tackle. Perhaps you had a starter outfit at one point, but now it's time to become more serious, more involved, and that requires a step up to better rods and reels.

Most surf regulars have a series of rods and reels geared to specific functions or times

of year. As winter gives way to spring, you'll see light 7- to 8-footers in use by anglers working the sod banks along coastal rivers in New Jersey, as well as by Rhode Islanders casting alongside Carpenters Bar on an April afternoon, intent not on 30-pounders but rather the first run of 14-inch schoolies fresh from their winter grounds. The little bass might not pull very hard, but they bend the rod and add zest to lives deprived of striped bass during the long, cold winter.

Several name-brand manufacturers turn out these light rods, rated for 8- to 15-pound line and lures up to an ounce or so. The sticks may run a bit shorter if used from some of the New Jersey jetties or perhaps a bit longer for situations requiring casting a half-ounce lead-head tipped with a soft-plastic worm out to the second wave off a likely-looking beach.

As the season moves on, shore anglers might change from the 7- to a 9-, 10- or 11-footer, rated beyond 2-ounce lures and lines to 20-pound as larger fish push up the coast. Today's graphite rods, produced in one or two pieces, are a joy to handle. They're ideal for lobbing a live eel out in the Shinnecock surf or tossing a bucktail with plastic worm into the current at Indian River Inlet.

If I were just entering my second or third season as a surfcaster, I'd opt for the 9-footer and see how it fit my needs. This is an easy-to-use length for the person of average height and weight. It can also be used to teach youngsters how to cast. Grade-schoolers, though, may need that 7-footer before graduating to something beyond their present physical stature.

I've watched proficient anglers tame 50-pound bass with 9-foot rods during the blitzes of the mid-1980s in the Block Island surf. During those years, many huge fish fell to black needlefish plugs, Rebels or live eels fished on that size rod. Several manufacturers now turn out one-piece 9-footers that cost a bit more, but these sticks will be around several years after the bargain-basement models have been relegated to the yard sale.

The 10-footer has sometimes been called the "one rod for the whole season." Anglers on a limited budget often buy that size rod to catch schoolies in the spring on seaworms and perhaps the last bluefish of the year by chucking Hopkins spoons into a Hatteras surf. This size rod will handle a 1-ounce plastic swimming plug, a 14-inch eel, or a 2-ounce popper. Excellent two-piece models are available for those who live in condos or have limited trunk space—it'll easily fit in the back of a Chevy or Lexus sedan.

Spinning reels to go with the 10-footer should hold 250 to 400 yards of 15- to 20-pound mono. Fifteen is the better starting choice unless you routinely work areas of snags and boulders. The lighter line will deliver longer casts to hit the outer bars found off almost all the sandy beaches from southern Maine to North Carolina.

The big boy of this section is the heavy-action 11-footer, used with 20- to 25-pound mono and the largest of today's salt water spinning reels. This rod will handle heavy metal spoons, big poppers and bait-dunking chores. Its extra length is sometimes a help when a trophy bass cranks up for its first frantic rush past a bunch of boulders in the wash. The 11-footer may just keep the line up out of harm's way where a 9-footer may not. A two-piece rod will be easier to store and transport, but lots of anglers tote several one-piecers of this length on the tops of their buggies or cars and profit from the extra casting distance the rod provides. The 11-footer will deliver a 3-ounce popper as far as most can toss and is able to lob a heavy pyramid sinker and chunk of bait out to fish that will not come up to smack a lure.

The 11-footer, while it has its place, is hard on us baby boomers with 30 years of surf-casting wear and tear on our shoulder muscles. While lightweight graphite construction may cut down on rod weight, casting with a 9-footer for six straight hours is easier on many of us.

At this point we might talk about conventional casting outfits, which consist of revolving-spool reels and heavy rods. Although not nearly as prevalent on the beaches today as spinning gear, these outfits nevertheless see increasing use by pros who like the power and muscle they can provide. On one side of the spectrum is the light 7-foot popping rod and small reel, used for casting lures to spring schoolies or for light bottom fishing. Going up the horsepower scale, we find 9-footers in use by some of the very sharp eel-slingers in

Rhode Island. One such individual immediately comes to mind. We call him "Eelman" because he casts live eels six nights per week with his trusty gold revolving-spool reel and 9-foot conventional-style rod. The six-nights-per-week figure isn't an exaggeration, because Eelman suffered a work injury and is now retired—at age 34! He has loads of time to fish and is a striped bass' worse nightmare.

Ten- and 11-foot conventional rods provide magnum power and can toss large plugs or bait rigs with sinkers heavy enough to stay put on the bottom beneath churning breakers. They work best with line from 20- to 30-pound test. One old-time, rigged-eel fisherman from Connecticut wouldn't be caught dead with a spinning outfit while going about his business at Cape Cod's Nauset Beach, much preferring his trusty 10-foot conventional rod coupled to his loyal Penn Squidder, a true workhorse of a surf reel for the past five decades.

Lures, Lures and More Lures

The intimidating wall of lures found in most coastal tackle shops may cause apprehension and a feeling of indecision. The choices seem endless. Your best course of action is to ask the shop owner for advice, especially if you are new to the area. What might be a killer lure along one section of the coast may be a dud along another. The topwater model always seems to work, be it the half-ounce, chrome model from Creek Chub that produces for surfcasters along Connecticut's western beaches to a variety of 1- to 2-ounce poppers that will take bass from Sandy Hook, New Jersey, to Delaware Bay. And no lure collection is complete without a couple ½- or 1-ounce plastic swimmers from Rebel, Bomber, Yo-Zuri, Redfin and Gags Grabbers. All have proven their worth along different sections of the striper coast. Metal lures such as Hopkins and Kastmasters are standard fare in sizes from 1 to 3 ounces. A newcomer of late to this category is the Crippled Herring from Luhr Jensen. It casts like a bullet, reaching fish out of range of other artificials. The lead-head bucktail jig is another staple. It caught bass in grandfather's day and still works as well in this new millennium. Add a

strip of pork rind or plastic curly-worm and you've got a striper-getter deluxe.

Probably the one category that has caught on the most during the late 1990s is that of the soft-plastic lures. From the Fin-S Fish and Slug-Go from Lunker City to a variety of shapes, sizes and colors made by Kalin or Andrus Lures, as well as the ubiquitous 6- to 10-inch plastic worm, these lures have duped untold thousands of bass—as well as blues and weakfish—from shore, and show every indication of continuing to do so in the future.

Accessories You Need

Time spent fishing the shoreline is better with good accessories. Rain gear is a must. Nobody ever made progress up the surf-fishing ladder without getting wet. It just goes with the territory. Most surf fishermen use some type of chest waders to go along with a rain jacket. Lightweight neoprene waders are gaining in popularity all the time, and are used with felt soles or Korkers, a tie-on shoe bottom with metal studs for negotiating slick rocks. It's no fun to slip and fall on a jetty at midnight and then have to try to make it ashore with a broken arm or worse. Safety first.

Some anglers, especially those who work jetties or rocky shorelines, prefer a rain jacket and bib pants worn over a pair of hip boots. A few others, notably the surf clan at Montauk and the south shore of Long Island, favor wet suits. They'll put them on, swim out to offshore rocks and catch a remarkable number of bass. While certainly a productive method, wet-suit casting is best postponed until you have a couple of years of surf fishing experience under your belt.

Other additions include a good neck light (with extra batteries and bulbs) for night work, a plug bag and some sort of pliers or line cutters. Plug bags come in all shapes and sizes—the bigger ones accommodate all the lures we *think* we need, but never do. If you can un-sling the bag and set it nearby while you fish, fine, but if your situation calls for it to be continually on your shoulder, select one that will tote the necessary lures but won't weigh you down. Pliers are indispensable for cutting line and removing hooks from fish. If you routinely work an area where there are likely to be bluefish mingling with the bass, consider needle-nose cutters; the extra jaw length is a help in removing swallowed plugs.

A baseball cap provides shade in summer, and a Navy-style watch cap keeps us bald-headed guys warm during the early spring and fall. Clothes under rain gear shouldn't be overdone or you'll sweat yourself into a chill and an early night home. Remember, you work up body heat while walking through the sand and casting. Plenty of today's fabrics allow the surf caster to enjoy his or her sport all season long in plenty of comfort.

Where to Find Bass

Striped bass thrive in areas where one current flows into another or where there's a break in a current in which they can lie quietly without expending undo energy yet still have a clear view of what's coming their way. You can use this simple rule to scout striper locations virtually anywhere along the East Coast.

These bass haunts, or edges, take many forms, including the white water created by incoming waves. As the surf hits a jetty, for example, it bounces off the side, sometimes causing a stream of white water to extend inshore at a 45-degree angle to the beach. Find the inside edge of the white water and you'll find bass. This was the situation at the Sixth Avenue jetty in Asbury Park, New Jersey (before the beach replenishment project altered the landscape), and the same condition currently exists at the inside edge of the white water at the reef off Southeast Light on Block Island during the top of a high tide. Edges can include the sides of a "bowl" on a sand beach or the fringes of some rocks along the same shore. You can look for bass at cuts in bars where water from the bowls runs in and out. Bass wait at the edge to feed or to use those areas as lanes to move inshore, possibly before the other, shallower areas of the outside bar have enough water depth to allow the bass to traverse them.

Bass also orient at the edge of a current break, such as the one at the mouth of Connecticut's Niantic River, on the east shore below the train bridge. Year after year, stripers

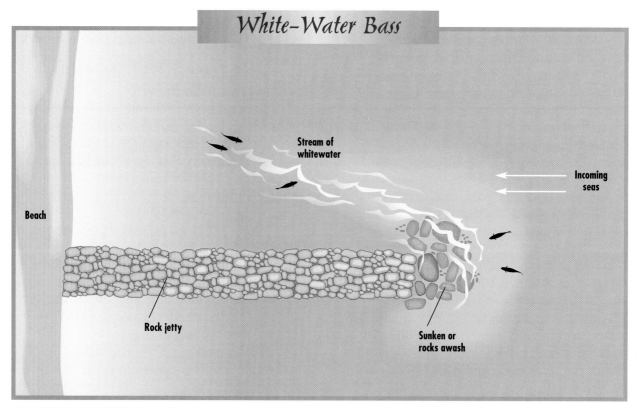

White-Water Bass

Stream of whitewater

Incoming seas

Beach

Rock jetty

Sunken or rocks awash

BASS LOVE WHITE WATER. You can find them on some jetties where oncoming seas break over sunken rocks, then sweep in toward the beach, creating a stream of white water at a 45-degree angle to the jetty. Locate the inside edge of this white water and you'll find bass.

lie in wait in the quiet water by the small rip that builds between shore and the tip of the eastern icebreaker. They'll hold near, but out of, the current in and around inlets along the Delmarva shore, in just the same types of spots they inhabit in New England and Cape May, New Jersey. Once you learn to spot an edge, you can take this knowledge on the road with you. The rock-bound sharpies of the Newport Saltwater Fishing Club in Rhode Island will find a second home along similar structure in Manchester and Gloucester, Massachusetts, and the sand-savvy surfmen of central Jersey have no problem scoring big bass during autumn trips to Nantucket.

Jetty Jockeying

This takes me back to 1964, when a novice threw a shiny blue-and-white Rebel plug into the wash from a jetty in New Jersey and watched in awe as a 6-pound striper followed, then grabbed the lure at the jetty's edge. The bass was released, but the caster—me—was hooked for life.

Jetties of all size and shape dot the striper's landscape up and down the shore. Some are only nubbins of rock extending a few yards into the wash, while others stretch a mile to protect a harbor from heavy seas. Each one has its own makeup, and each one harbors bass at some time or another. The small rockpile might have a fish worth catching at daybreak at a time of month when tides are fullest. The end of the mile-long breakwall might be the place on an outgoing tide as all the bait in the harbor is flushed seaward. In between are jetties like the ones on the bay side of Cape Cod, often worked by casters to salvage a weekend when a storm has roiled the water on the ocean side.

One area of any jetty worth attention is the pocket between the jetty and shore. The first time I ever fished the East Wall of Point Judith, Rhode Island, was back in 1973, with a live herring tossed in by the large boulder that becomes awash at low water. The herring hadn't swum 10 feet when a 41-pound bass abandoned its position by the rock to take up another—on the scales at Top Of The Dock

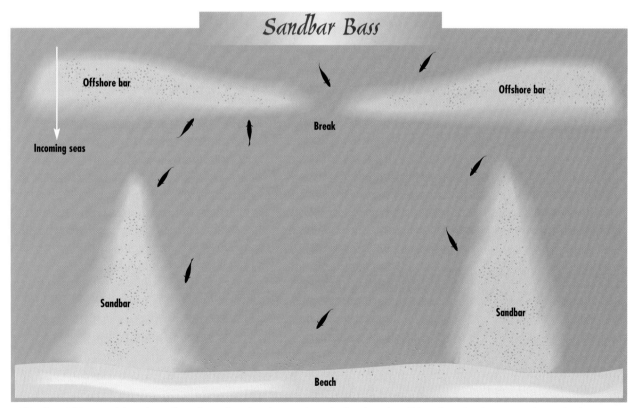

Sandbar Bass

Offshore bar

Offshore bar

Break

Incoming seas

Sandbar

Sandbar

Beach

LOOK FOR BASS around the edges of sandbars along beaches or along the break in the offshore bars that bass use either as feeding station or highway depending on the lay of the land.

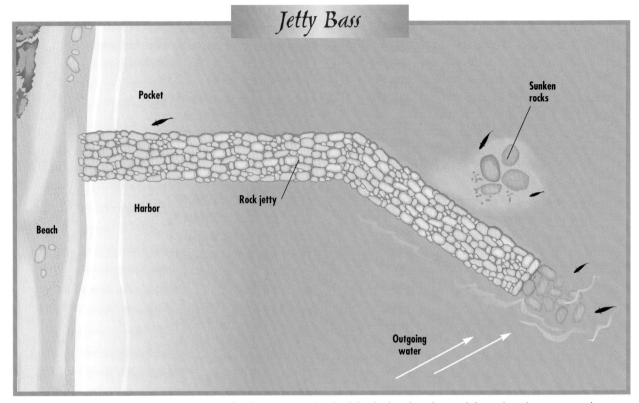

ON A LONG JETTY protecting a harbor, you might find bass in the pocket back by the beach and around the end on the outgoing tide.

bait shop. Some jetties have holes in them where one body of water washes through to another. The famed South Jetty at Barnegat Inlet, New Jersey, was like that until it was rebuilt sometime after 1972. The water from the bay would wash through the jetty holes and into the ocean, creating a small rip that bass used to their advantage. Find a similar situation and you can enjoy success. Another jetty locale always worth investigating is the tip, be it bordering a tidal river or just the open surf at daybreak. Ask any New Jersey jetty jockey how many bass have been taken off the tips of the North Jersey jetties at sunrise on plugs.

Inlets

Find one body of water washing into another and you have an inlet, a place where stripers like to dine. An inlet can be as tiny as a two-foot-wide stream flowing out into a tidal river, bringing bait to spring schoolies, or it can be as wide across as the Narrow River in Rhode Island, dumping herring out to bass

that line up in the rip on the last few hours of late-May tides. Boat traffic can be heavy during the day, but come the quiet of a late-night dropping tide, bass of all sizes watch and wait at various junction points along the base of the inlet's jetties for edible tidbits to be washed to them.

Case in point: Expert fisherman Al Williams of Gloucester, Massachusetts, is a real pro when it comes to taking huge stripers to 63 pounds from his boat in the waters from Baker's Island to Straitsmouth Light. But the largest bass he ever hooked came not from his boat, but from shore at night, at the mouth of the Blynman Canal, the busy water-artery between Ipswich Bay and Gloucester Harbor. Al had flipped a live eel into the current and hooked a bass that, by his best estimate after 20 years of experience, was well into the mid-60-pound range. Unfortunately the fish won that round, but inlets are now high on Al's priority list.

While inlets are known for productivity on the falling tide, many of them produce as well on an incoming flow. The West Wall jetty

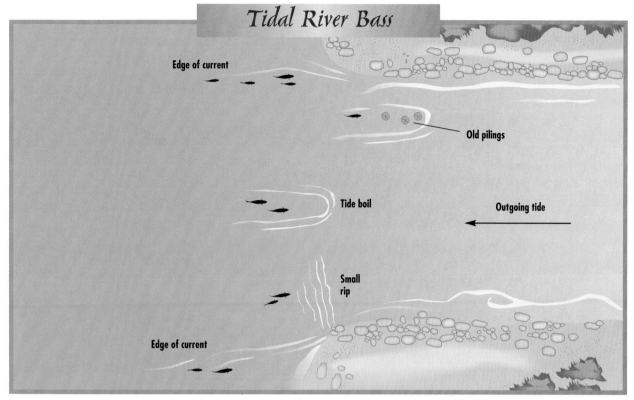

Tidal River Bass

Edge of current

Old pilings

Tide boil

Outgoing tide

Small rip

Edge of current

STRIPERS HANG AROUND EDGES in the surf zone. These can be the edge of a current or various types of structure the fish use to their advantage.

of Rhode Island's Point Judith Harbor is known to the locals as a place to land a 30-pounder on a jig-and-worm or jig-and-pork-rind on the last hour or so of the flood tide. June anglers in Quonochontaug Breachway (Rhode Island's name for an inlet) line up at the entrance of the breach into Quonnie Pond. The flow of one body of water into another brings bass to the jetty and shore, within range of a caster equipped with a plastic swimmer or eel at night, or perhaps a popper at dawn.

Sometimes catching fish in an inlet is as simple as tossing a swimming plug seaward and then reeling it back while bracing for the hit. At other inlets plugs are floated out into the tide, then retrieved after being carried seaward a specific distance measured by counting seconds. The count ensures continuity of drifts if fish are lying in one portion of the current. After casting, you count to, say, five, and then start a retrieve. On the next cast you count to ten, and so on until you get a hit. Some inlets where this type of fishing is practiced can get crowded, so anglers fish in

rotation. One angler casts and lets his lure run out, then the next caster follows suit. Casters who favor bucktails fish their offerings in a similar manner, watching as the lure swings in an arc from 45 degrees up into the current to 45 degrees down-tide.

Inlets with a lot of debris on the bottom present a problem, as lures continually become snagged. For those spots, another method, the "dropback," presents itself. You'll need water depth between 15 and 30 feet. Arrive just as the tide starts to ebb. Cast a 1-ounce lead-head, dressed with bucktail and pork rind or soft-plastic trailer, at a 45-degree angle across and down into the tide. As the lure hits the water, keep the reel in free-spool, letting the lure drop to the bottom. (You'll need a conventional reel for this, as you must control the spin of the spool with one hand, yet be able to feel for the lure hitting bottom with the other as the line runs through your fingers.) As soon as the lure hits bottom, put the reel in gear, then take five slow turns of the handle. What happens is that the lure touches bottom, then begins to rise and move

off to the side. A bass watching this must make up its mind in a hurry—or lose out on dinner. If you don't connect after the first five turns, take the reel out of gear again and let the lure drop back once more. As soon as it touches down, put the reel back in gear and begin again. On some inlets, this second dropback puts the lure right at the base of the jetty rocks—always a good spot—or perhaps into a pocket out of the main current created by a bend in the jetty. You can continually do this until the lure is too far away for you to effectively set the hook if you get a strike.

Smart inlet fishermen bring two or three sizes of bucktails and use heavier or lighter ones as the current increases or decreases, repectively. The lightest lure that will reach the bottom is the one that is most effective on bass. A 1-ounce jig in a strong tidal current isn't the best choice, but a 2- or even 3-ounce model might work fine. Conversely, as the tide eases, decrease the weight of the jig to compensate for less tidal movement.

Bait on the Bottom

Many surf and shore anglers have caught the striped bass of their dreams by simply fishing bait on bottom. How many times has a local newspaper recounted the tale of a Sunday family beach trip that turned into a shouting match as the kids in their bathing suits jumped up and down, yelling, trying to direct dad's attention to the rod doubled over in the sand spike with a 60-pound bass attached to the business end of the line?

The basic bait rig is made up of a three-way swivel with a metal clip holding a pyramid sinker of enough weight to hold bottom. A 30- to 36-inch section of mono leader, attached to a hook of choice, is tied to the second eye of the swivel. The end of the fishing line is tied to the third eye.

Most coastal tackle shops offer these rigs ready-made to conform to local conditions. Along the Jersey shore you might find the "doodlebug," a bottom rig designed to fish a small, whole mullet or other baitfish. New Englanders buy any number of pre-fabricated rigs on which to dunk their pogy (menhaden), herring or mackerel chunks. On those occasions when these three popular baits are not available, some savvy anglers borrow a page from the tuna chunker and use butterfish, often sold by the dozen in freezer packs or by the flat if a whole weekend's worth of chunks are needed.

While the pyramid sinker is the standard design for the surf and sandy bottom, some anglers opt for the bank style, which will roll around and get the bait chunks to move about in the wash or waves, providing a more natural presentation. Another rig that offers a natural presentation is called the fishfinder rig, which consists of a plastic sleeve through which the line is threaded. The sinker is attached to the sleeve via a clip. The advantage of this rig is that a striper can pick up the bait and move off, pulling the line through the sleeve without dragging the sinker and feeling resistance.

No discussion of bait fishing is complete without mention of seaworms and squid. Not as popular perhaps as they once were, these baits nevertheless catch striped bass. Ask any Cape Cod surf veteran how many jumbo bass have been taken on seaworms, or ask the guys who used to fish the rocky perches of Little Compton, Rhode Island, how many 50-pounders have fallen for squid cast seaward on bait rigs.

Ready-made rigs to fish worms are available at many bait shops. They feature a three-way swivel, a sinker clip, a leader onto which two hooks have been snelled, and a bright red cork that acts as an attractor and also floats the worms off the bottom and away from crabs and other scavengers. Some sharpies make their supply of natural worms go further by adding a scented plastic worm to one of the hooks along with the real thing.

End Game

Perhaps the culmination of all the effort and expense is realized on the magic night or bleary sunrise or dusk when the sun sinks below layers of ominous clouds and the rod bends double with the jolting strike of a trophy bass. Bringing that fish ashore, to admire it in the moonlight or daylight, makes all the tired muscles, red eyes and hours of casting worthwhile. Sometimes the magic occurs very early in one's surf career, but for many others, years of vigilance are needed to break that barrier. It took me 19 seasons of hungry searching, fishing harder than some, to beach a 47-pounder. Then one week, late in my 20th season, all the credits came due when fish of 50 and 54½ pounds struck on successive casts at 3:00 a.m. on a November morning. Four nights later, a 51-pounder inhaled my black needlefish plug.

One year and a day later to the day, a 67-pounder grabbed my plug, and put me, my reel and my 10-foot conventional rod to the ultimate test. That fish now resides on my wall, a reminder that, in fishing, dreams can actually come true.

—*Tim Coleman*

BASIC FLY FISHING FOR STRIPED BASS

Stripers consistently feed on small baits that are ideal to match with flies.

In the last five years fly fishing for stripers has become very popular. The striper's size and availability offer opportunities for many fly anglers. There are large numbers of stripers in the 4- to 12-pound range that live in waters reachable in any size boat, from small runabouts to large offshore craft. Many of the major cities have fishable populations of stripers right in the shadows of their buildings.

Stripers are ideal fish to catch on fly tackle. Most of the time they take flies aggressively. The only exception is when stripers move into shallow, clear water in the daytime. They live in a variety of water types, feeding on many kinds of prey, both large and small.

Stripers consistently feed on small baits that are ideal to match with flies. There are times when feeding stripers will frustrate the conventional angler, but the fly-rodder, using a small fly, can hook fish after fish.

Sand eels, anchovies, crabs and shrimp are just some of the small foods that the fly angler can match with flies. There is no lure I know, other than a fly, that looks alive just sitting in the water with no added action from the angler.

Fly fishing is not difficult, just different. The angler must realize that a fly rod does not produce the same casting distance one achieves with spin tackle. The trade-off is how a fly comes alive in the water and how a fly entices a fish into striking. I have had days on my boat when I drove spin anglers nuts because the fish were only feeding on tiny baits, or only taking a fly because of its pulsating action.

Fly-Fishing Equipment

Fly Rods

Most salt water fly rods manufactured today are made of a graphite composite. Older glass fly rods will work, but they are comparatively heavy and do not perform nearly as well as today's high-tech models. There are many quality rods available in a wide range of prices; even the modestly priced rods will perform for most anglers.

The 9-foot fly rod is a standard striper size, but some manufacturers are making rods of 8 or 8½ foot, designed especially for boat fishing. A shorter rod is easier to manipulate in the confined quarters of a boat, and extra rod length is not necessary as it is when wading. However, the 9-foot rod is still the workhorse, and this length is available in many models.

When choosing fly tackle, there are several considerations. The most important is the types of locations you plan to fish. When fishing mostly sheltered areas, flats or places without heavy current, a number 8- or 9-weight rod will work well. If fishing big offshore rips with large flies, a rod with more lifting and casting power, like a number 10- or 11-weight, is a better choice.

What type of angler will be using the tackle? If it is a family outfit, the lighter 8-weight will be better suited for women and kids. Eight- and 9-weights are very popular with the casual fly-rodder, but the 9-weight is the most popular.

A mid- or medium-action rod is a good choice for most anglers. Rods that have fast actions, or are too stiff, require a longer line to load the rod when casting. Faster rods are more difficult to handle for the beginner. If you are having difficulty feeling the line when casting, try using a fly line that is one size larger than the rod is rated for. Overloading a rod with a slightly heavier fly line helps the rod bend more, making casting easier.

The rod should have a strong, noncorrosive reel seat with a 1- to 2-inch fighting butt extending from the back of the reel seat. Look for a large stripping guide and large snake guides and tip-top. This will allow minor line tangles to pass through the guides. Two-piece rods are less expensive, but for easy storage, four-piece rods are hard to beat. Do not worry about the strength of multi-piece rods, as modern ferrules are well-designed and strong.

Reels

There are several types of fly reels on the market—single-action, anti-reverse, large-arbor and multipliers. Single-action reels are the least expensive and come in a wide range of models. These reels are the choice of most anglers. A reel with an exposed spool rim allows the angler to control the drag with hand pressure by pressing on the bottom of the reel when a fish runs. If you are a doctor, musician or jeweler an anti-reverse reel will help protect your hands—the handle does not spin when the fish runs. Both the multiplier and large-arbor reels retrieve line more quickly than a standard-type reel.

A single-action reel that holds 150 yards of 30-pound-test Dacron backing, plus a fly line, is sufficient for most striper fishing. Only if you are planning to fish offshore

A FIGHTING BUTT allows you to place the end of the rod against your body for extra fighting leverage.

SINGLE-ACTION FLY REELS with exposed spool rims are the most popular for stripers.

rips where you cannot safely chase a big fish, or to also use the fly tackle for other, larger, faster species would I recommend a bigger reel. Stripers make powerful runs, but they lack the speed of the tuna-type fish. Select a reel with a strong frame and a sound, non-corrosive drag. There is a good selection of fly reels in the $100 to $300 price range.

Fly reels are easy to change from right- to left-hand retrieve. There are many opinions regarding the correct hand to use when reeling while fighting a fish. My advice is to use the hand that is your best reeling hand. Most right-handed spin anglers reel with their left hand; why change because you are fly fishing? Also, if you reel with the non-casting hand, you never need to change hands when fighting a fish.

Set the reel drag to about a 3- to 4-pound straight pull off the reel. Be sure to check the drag for smoothness before each use. If a fly reel sits for several days, salt can gum up a drag.

Fly Lines

Floating fly lines are easiest to cast, but they are not always the most effective. The most versatile fly line is the intermediate weight-forward. It will cast well and sink just enough to avoid the wind and get the fly down in a slow rip. The intermediate fishes a variety of water depths; in slow current you can get the fly down to about 5 feet.

The clear intermediate is a good choice for sight casting to fish in shallow, clear water. The intermediate will fish a mid-size popper fairly well. If you are mostly surface fishing, then a floating or an Orvis 10-foot Clear-Sink-Tip is a good choice. The Clear Tip line is ideal for sight casting and fishes a popper well, and the 10-foot intermediate tip will get the fly down better than a floater.

Fast-sinking lines are a necessity when fishing fast, deep water. The Teeny Depth Charge type line, which has a very fast-sinking 30-foot front section and a floating or intermediate running line, is ideal for the angler who fishes offshore rips. In just several outings most anglers can learn to work these lines effectively. These lines are the choice of most guides who fish deep holes, fast drop-offs along shorelines, and fast-flowing rips.

Leaders

A standard knotless tapered leader 7½ to 9 feet long is the best way to keep fly fishing simple. With a permanent loop at the fly line's

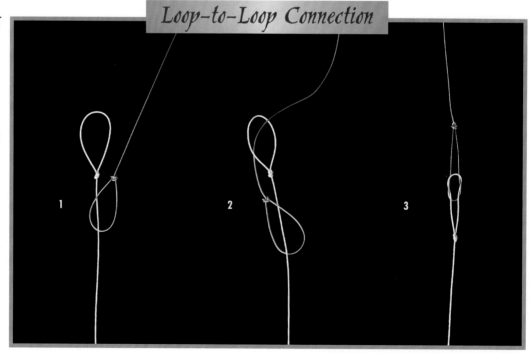

PASS LOOP IN FIRST SECTION (white) through loop in second section (blue) (1). Thread other end of second section through loop in first (2). Pull standing parts of both sections until knot snugs up (3).

Loop-to-Loop Connection

1   2   3

end, adding a leader is simple and takes little time. Many fly line companies offer a leader-to-line loop attached to the end of the fly line. This allows the angler to attach a tapered leader to the fly line without tying a knot by just interlocking the loop on the fly line to the loop on the tapered leader. This simple leader system is easy to use, requiring one knot to attach the fly and one knot to add tippet material as the leader shortens with use.

For most striper fishing I use a 16-pound tippet. In heavy rips, or for fishing around structure, 20-pound is a better choice. In the last several years fluorocarbon has become my favorite tippet material. It is very durable, lasts much longer than most monofilament, and is less visible underwater.

To tie on the fly, use a twice-through-the-eye clinch or an improved clinch knot, both of which have 95% knot strength. To add tippet material to the leader use a double surgeon's knot (p. 42). Be sure to use tippet material that knots well to the tapered leader. Different types of monofilaments do not always marry well, and fluorocarbon will not knot to some monofilaments. The safest leader system is one that uses the same type of material from the same manufacturer.

One other item to add to the leader system is a bite guard. Bluefish and bass will feed together, and if you start to lose flies to the cutting teeth of bluefish, a short wire leader will help prevent cut-offs. Several manufacturers make light wire leaders, 4 to 8 inches long, with either a small snap or a retwistable device that has a plastic tube on one end and a small loop on the other. Simply tie the tippet to the small loop on the bite guard, as you would tie on a fly, then snap on the fly. In clear water, wire leaders can be poison to stripers, so if you must use a bite guard use a short, thin one.

The Line System

The better fly shops and fly tackle companies set up the entire line system for the angler. If you must repair the system or add a fly line, you only need a nail knot or tube knot (p. 104). Both connections—the backing to the fly line and the loop to the end of the fly line—require a nail knot to finish the connection. I use a drop of super glue on both knots

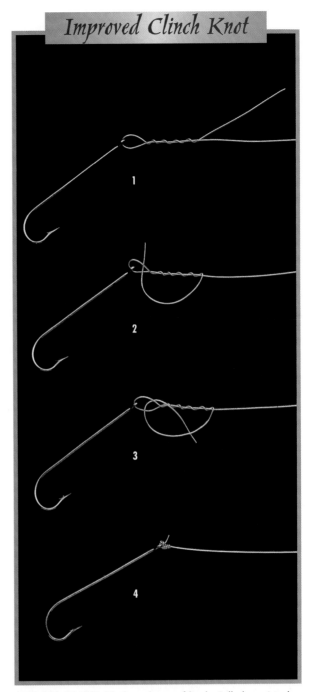

Improved Clinch Knot

PASS END OF LINE (1) through eye of hook. Pull about 6 inches of line through and double it back against itself. Twist five to seven times. (2) Pass end of the line through the small loop formed just above the eye, (3) then through the big loop just created. Be careful coils don't overlap. (4) Pull tag end and main line so that coiled line tightens against the eye. Again, be careful coils haven't overlapped. Trim excess.

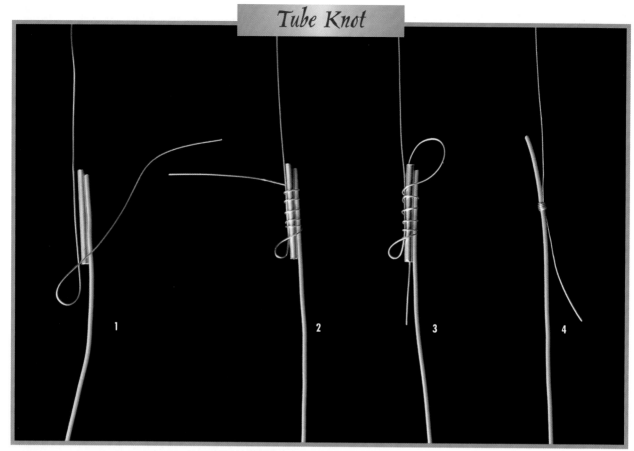

Tube Knot

PLACE HOLLOW TUBE alongside fly line and loop butt end of leader alongside tube (1), as shown. Wrap butt end around tube, fly line and standing part of leader five to six times (2). Pass butt though tube as shown (3). Carefully remove tube. Pull tag end and standing part of leader until knot is just snug. Tighten knot slowly (4), using your fingernails to position wraps evenly before tightening completely. Closely trim tag ends.

to insure a better hold and longer life. I use 30-pound-test Dacron backing for all my systems; 20-pound is less durable and has much lower (backing to fly line) knot strength.

Tackle Care

Most salt water fly tackle is corrosion free, and a simple hosing down with fresh water will keep the gear running. Some drag systems require special care, so consult the owner's manual before just spraying them with oil. WD-40 is a good general lubricant because it is fish-oil-based and will not add an offensive smell. Fly line and backing are highly absorbent, so be sure when applying spray-on lubricants to avoid getting any spray on the fly line and backing.

A dirty fly line is prone to tangle. Clean the line with mild soap and warm water or use a line cleaner.

Before Fishing

There are several important duties to perform before each outing. Stretch the fly line to remove the coils that form when the line sits on the reel. These coils will make casting difficult and cause knotting problems when a fish runs. If the fly line is not straightened, the line might tangle at the first guide when a fish runs, breaking the leader.

Always check the leader and knot connections for wear and the tippet for wind knots. A wind knot can weaken the tippet by 50 percent. Either remove the wind knot or change the leader.

One piece of equipment that is very useful is a stripping basket. Although used mostly for wading, it will work well in a boat to prevent the fly line from catching on numerous snags, including your feet.

Best Flies and How to Fish Them

As there are many different patterns, I will only mention a few of the names of the best-known flies. In some cases I will just mention the bait type with a description of the fly and let you choose a matching pattern.

Most of the time simple attractor flies, patterns tied with active materials that are 2 to 5 inches long, will catch fish. I use flies with materials like saddle hackle, marabou and Krystal Flash about 70 percent of the time. I fish with precise patterns, flies that look lifelike, and small patterns about 30 percent of the time. Flies in solid colors of white, black and chartreuse work well in many situations, and for the part-time fly rodder a simple selection of attractor flies will cover most bases.

There are some guidelines to follow when selecting color. On bright days, over light-colored bottoms or in clear water, fish a light-colored fly. On dark days, over dark bottoms or in discolored water, fish a dark-colored fly. Even at night, if the moon is bright and the water is clear, fish a light-colored fly. On dark nights black flies work well. Remember, these are only basic guidelines—keep changing color and size until you find the right combination.

The size and weight of the fly pattern are important considerations. Big, bulky or heavy flies are hard to cast, particularly with a light-weight fly outfit. Take a hard look at your casting skills before buying large flies and poppers. Even a good caster can have difficulty tossing a 9-inch menhaden pattern with an 8-weight fly outfit. A 10- or 11-weight outfit is a better choice if you plan to fish larger flies.

In early spring big baitfish and squid move in to spawn; the month of May to the first part of June is a good time for big flies in some locations. June also begins the influx of smaller baitfish that have hatched and will keep growing till fall. The fall run will see numbers of 2- to 6-inch herring and menhaden, plus 4- to 6-inch sand eels and spearing.

Important Fly Patterns

The most popular striper fly is the Lefty's Deceiver. Tied in different variations and sizes, it can imitate many baits. A 5-inch white Deceiver has probably hooked more stripers than any other fly pattern. A Deceiver is a neutral-density fly; it suspends in the water, holding at a given depth. If tied sparsely it matches a spearing; heavily dressed it is a good herring or bunker pattern.

A Deceiver is effective in a rip. Cast it downcurrent on an angle across the flow, retrieving the fly with short, hard pulls so it flows across the current and turns upcurrent at the end of the retrieve. A Deceiver has good pulsating action because the materials keep moving even when the fly stops moving, so it looks alive even while drifting without forward motion. Short, hard pulls excite stripers, making the fly look like a crippled baitfish. Also, try fishing the fly with long, fast pulls and a pause of several seconds between each pull.

Current speed can, at times, determine the speed of retrieve. In slower water move the fly more quickly; in a fast flow use a slow retrieve or let the fly just swing, drifting in the flow, without retrieving. Another factor that will determine fly speed is the manner in which the fish are feeding. When fish are crashing the surface and feeding aggressively, move the fly quickly. If fish are just cruising, making small dimples on the surface, move the fly very slowly.

The Snake Fly is also an attractor pattern and perhaps my favorite. It duplicates sand eels, spearing, cinder worms and eels. I fish it much like a Deceiver, but it will act differently because of its design. The fly is buoyant, so it will dart toward the surface after each pull when fished with a sinking line. The flared deer hair head makes it wiggle like a snake when retrieved with short, quick pulls. The wiggling action is the key to this fly's success. Fished on a floating line, a Snake Fly will form a good surface wake on flat water that is very effective on calm water in low light.

Tabory's Snake Fly

Lefty's Deceiver

The Clouser Minnow is a very popular pattern designed to ride hook-up to minimize snagging the bottom. This fly, tied with heavy weighted eyes, simulates the hopping action of a bucktail jig. Use a stop-and-go action of different speeds to make the fly hop. The bouncing action makes this fly very effective. However, a heavily weighted fly tied with little material is difficult, and at times dangerous, to cast. These flies tend to soar around like an errant missile and inflict welts or worse upon anglers who are not smooth casters. Remember, a fly can travel at over 100 miles per hour and will hit like a pellet fired from an air rifle. Lightly weighted Clousers work well, so unless you are a smooth caster, avoid any fly that makes a loud clunk when dropped onto a glass counter!

Clouser Minnow

Skipping Bug

Poppers are effective on calm days if you use a slow retrieve with lots of splash. Stripers will rise up from the depths or travel some distance to slam a popper. Casting a popper into breaking fish should bring an immediate strike.

When working a popper—and for that matter any fly—on surface feeding fish, move it quickly. Make the fish see the fly. Sometimes a slow-moving lure goes unnoticed when fish are actively feeding on the surface. Choose a popper that you can cast and can see. I generally fish yellow or white poppers

but also have a few dark blue or black ones for fishing in low light. Even a small popper will make a good splash; with a popper you can make a small offering appear big.

When a popper does not work in breaking fish there is probably too much natural bait in the area. Sand eels massed in thick schools near the surface cause a feeding frenzy that will drive fish and anglers crazy. When fish feed in thick sand eels they can be difficult, and sometimes impossible, to catch. Usually there is just too much competition for your offering. This is when a simple sand eel fly can turn frustration into fantastic fishing. Sand eel patterns are 2- to 5-inch flies with small tails, no wings and swizzle stick-to-pencil size-bodies. Use solid-colored flies or try some lifelike multi colored variations with epoxy bodies. I use epoxy even on plain black sand eel flies so they sink. In thick schools of sand eels, fish the fly below the suspended bait, concentrating on the stripers that are feeding on the dead and crippled sand eels as they drift down.

In thick schools of baitfish, some stripers rush through with their mouths open, not selecting individual baitfish. These fish kill and cripple many baitfish that they do not eat.

Tabory's Sand Lance

Casting and working the fly slowly below the heavy concentration of bait is the best way to take fish in thick sand eels. Here the stripers will single out your fly because it looks like a wounded bait. Many times the bigger fish feed below, knowing that they will eat well without working for their food.

The Surf Candy is a lifelike fly pattern designed to match spearing and anchovies. It has an epoxy body with a stiff tail; in your hand this fly looks like a real baitfish. In clear

Surf Candy

Bunker Fly

water, use a stop-and-go retrieve to make the fly look injured. Around schools of bait, use a slow retrieve, letting the fly slowly flutter below the bait, the same way you fish under a school of sand eels.

To match big baits such as herring and menhaden, a large Deceiver pattern works well.

Again, select flies that you can cast. When big bait are stunned they swim slowly, with a darting motion. Make the fly glide, stop, then hold for a short time before moving the fly again. An erratic action works well with big flies.

Use a Slab (Bunker) Fly or small Deceiver from the late summer into the fall when there are large numbers of juvenile herring and menhaden present. These baits move quickly, so use a fast retrieve, or try a slow stop-and-go right near or under thick schools of bait.

In May squid move into the offshore rips and along beaches to spawn. This bait, in some areas, can provoke heavy feeding and hold stripers in a location for some time. Use one of the many squid patterns, or just fish a Deceiver or Snake Fly in all white. Squid glide, stop and hold, flowing through the water with a spinning motion. They are very fast. Use

long, sharp pulls, then let the fly pause for several seconds. At times, let the fly swing with the current and make short pulls without taking in line. This retrieve also works well in a fast current with big flies.

Crabs and shrimp are important food for stripers in shallow water. Choose crab patterns about the size of a quarter and shrimp flies 1 to 2 inches long. Most of the time you are casting in clear, shallow water to a sighted, moving fish. Place the fly ahead of the fish, then let it settle to the bottom so the fish sees it. In most cases the fish will rush the fly, taking it either on the drop or off the bottom. Like bonefishing, this type of angling is becoming very popular with striper anglers.

Del's Merkin Crab

Popovic's Ultra Shrimp

Martha's Vineyard Squid Fly

Retrieving, Hooking and Fighting Fish

There are two ways to retrieve a fly—the one-handed and two-handed methods. I use a two-handed retrieve with the rod tucked under my casting arm. I move the fly with a hand-over-hand motion, retrieving as you would when pulling an anchor line. If you prefer to hold the rod while retrieving, pinch the line between the cork handle with the first finger of your casting hand, pulling the line with the non-casting hand. Use whatever retrieve is most comfortable. The two-handed retrieve is more popular.

The biggest mistake fly anglers make is trying to hook a fish by raising the rod. When a fish hits, keep retrieving until the line tightens. If using a two-handed retrieve, use both hands to hook the fish with a straight pull on the line. With a single-handed retrieve, pull with both the rod hand and retrieving hand toward your body. Striking with the rod can

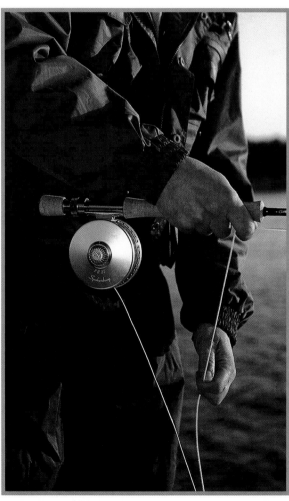

ONE-HANDED RETRIEVE allows the angler to hold the rod while retrieving by pinching the line between the cork handle with the first finger of your casting hand and pulling the line with the non-casting hand.

TWO-HANDED RETRIEVE requires placing the rod under the casting arm and moving the fly with a hand-over-hand motion.

break the rod or the tippet and remove the fly from the fish's range if you miss the strike. With the rod tucked under your arm you will never make this mistake.

Once the fish is hooked, let it run freely until the line is flowing off the reel. Then raise the rod to about a 45-degree angle, applying pressure only with the bottom half of the rod. The tip half of the rod should be straight if you're fighting the fish properly. Do not hold the rod high. A high rod position applies little pressure to the fish, and once the fish nears the boat it can break the rod.

To gain line on the fish after it stops running, lift with the rod, pumping the fish in, then reel in the line while dropping the rod. Be sure to keep the rod low, never over that 45-degree angle. Once the fish is below the boat, the rod tip should be in the water when the angler lifts the fish, unless the angler is standing well above the water. For small fish that do not run, hold the rod at the fighting angle, pinch the line to the rod and strip the fish in with the non-casting hand.

Our striper fishery with fly tackle offers excellent opportunities for all levels of anglers. Stripers are ideal fly-rod fish because they live and feed in such a variety of waters and take flies aggressively. I feel stripers are one of the best fly-rod fish in the sea.

—Lou Tabory

Fly Fishing from Shore

One of the most exciting ways to catch striped bass is from shore with a fly rod. You can either wade to the fish if the water is shallow, or find spots with deep water close to the bank. Your biggest challenge is finding a spot that not only holds fish, but is within casting range. If you find such an area where the water is clear, you can even sight-cast to stripers!

Most sheltered beaches are ideal for wading. Look for shorelines offering easy walking. Beaches with sand or sand mixed with small, fist-size stones are best. Novices should avoid ocean beaches with heavy surf, or rock strewn shorelines.

Many shallow beaches are easier to fish on foot than from a boat. Wading anglers can quietly work in close, fishing those small hard-to-reach pockets not available to boating anglers. A good time to fish these shorelines is during low-light conditions and after dark. The fish are close to shore and often feeding aggressively.

When fly fishing from shore, you don't have the luxury of following a big fish after it's hooked, which is one reason I like to fish with heavy fly tackle. I prefer a reel with at least 200 yards of 30-pound backing and a rod that is 9 to 9 ½ feet long designed for a 9- to 10-weight fly line. In a boat you can carry several outfits and use a lighter rod when conditions permit; when wading, however, you need to plan for strong winds, rough water and hard-to-reach fish, all of which require beefy tackle.

You'll want to travel light for this type of fishing, so carry a small tackle bag or chest pack with extra flies, leaders and other gear.

To maximize your casting distance from shore, use a stripping basket. Even in calm, slow-moving water a floating fly line is tough to lift from the water's surface. Sinking lines are almost impossible to cast without a basket.

Boot-foot waders are the best choice for shore fishing. They keep you warm, dry and allow you to fish comfortably for long periods of time in nasty conditions. If the areas you fish have rugged, broken, rocky bottoms you'll need waders featuring heavy-duty wading boots. You should also own a pair of strap-on metal-studded soles, called "creepers," for walking on slippery, rocky bottoms.

Some small-boat anglers combine wading with boat fishing, using the boat to reach locations with no shore access or areas that require a long walk. Usually the boat is anchored while you wade to the fish. This works well when fishing flats that require a careful approach. By walking slowly and quietly into these areas you can have some hot fishing, especially at night.

There are also many productive shoreline areas where you can simply park your vehicle, walk a beach without stepping into the water, and catch feeding fish. These are ideal places when you're pressed for time but want to experience the thrill of battling a striped bass on fly gear.

SOME SMALL-BOAT ANGLERS combine wading with boat fishing, using the boat to reach locations with no shore access or areas that require a long walk.

Trophy Fishing for
STRIPED BASS

TROPHY FISHING FOR STRIPED BASS

SEARCH FOR A TROPHY

I t's the million-dollar question: How do I catch a really big striped bass? The truth is, there's no quick and easy formula. Unless you hire a charter captain or guide, you're going to have to put in some time searching and experimenting until you crack the code for your home waters. Now for the good news. Even though trophy stripers are elusive, there are several fundamental ways to improve your chances of finding and bagging one; keep them in mind throughout the season.

Think Deep

Ask a successful charter captain what his top recommendation for targeting trophy striped bass would be, and chances are he'd say to fish deep, right near the bottom. Whether you do this with wire line, sinkers, downriggers or heavy jigs, getting your bait or lure to where the fish are holding is usually the key to success. Of course, it's possible to catch big bass on or near the surface at certain times (for example, during the spring and fall migrations) and in certain places (i.e., in the surf), but the majority of truly large fish are taken on or near the bottom. This is especially true once the stripers have settled into their summer haunts, and if you do most of your fishing during the day.

One reason large stripers are found near the bottom is that they like to orient themselves around structure, which they use as ambush sites and to shield themselves from strong currents. Also, many types of striper prey (such as eels and lobsters) live in and around bottom structure.

Another reason concerns water temperature. As the water grows warmer in summer, the fish move to deeper, cooler areas that are within their comfort range. The hotter the weather, the deeper you're likely to find the fish. In recent years, schools of truly giant bass have even been discovered in water well over 100 feet deep. Deep water also offers reduced light levels, which bass prefer.

Fishing deep also applies when you encounter a school of fish feeding on the surface. Whether the fish on top are bluefish or small stripers, try fishing a bait or lure near the bottom. Often, the largest stripers lurk below, patiently waiting to pick off injured baits or fish bits that filter down to them. The trick, of course, is getting your offering past the more aggressive surface fish, which can be

Unless you hire a charter captain or guide, you're going to have to put in a lot of time searching and experimenting.

done by using a bait or lure that's too big for the small guys to eat; sending down a fast-sinking jig; trolling around the edge of the school with wire line, downriggers or deep-swimming plugs; or sneaking a natural bait past the dinks with a heavy sinker.

Fish the Prime Time

Trophy stripers wait for no man, which is why you often have to fish at such ungodly hours to catch them. Anyone the least familiar with striper fishing knows that dawn is prime time, which means being on the water or on the beach just as the eastern horizon begins to brighten, a period also known as false dawn. This is when stripers of all sizes feed most actively, and when you generally have your best shot at catching them in the upper portions of the water column and on the surface—particularly important if you like to throw surface lures or flies. The window of opportunity is often a matter of an hour—sometimes less, especially during the middle of the season—but it can yield some tremendous catches. As at dawn, stripers also frequently stage a feeding blitz just as the sun dips below the horizon at dusk.

During mid-season (July and August), particularly in the northern reaches of the striper's migratory range, night is the best time to search for a trophy, especially if you fish from shore or use fly gear. Under the cover of darkness, some very large fish will often move into surprisingly shallow water in search of a meal.

Follow the (Big) Bait

Big fish like big bait, and where there's an abundance of the latter, you will usually find the former. Acquaint yourself with the major migrations of large baitfish in your region and be ready to roll when they occur. A side benefit of using big baits is that they select for larger fish, which means you won't have to spend a lot of time tangling with schoolies in your search for that one monster bass.

Each spring in the Northeast, blueback herring and alewives migrate into rivers and streams in order to spawn, and hot on their heels are large stripers. Find out when the herring are "in," then get yourself a batch of live ones and fish them at dawn near the mouth of a local run. This is an excellent time to take some very large fish in shallow water, and even big flies and topwater plugs produce. If you can't obtain live baits, drift-fish some fresh-dead herring on the bottom or jig them on a sliding-sinker (fishfinder) rig over deep structure such as rocks and sandbars in the neighborhood of the run. Slow-trolling herring-sized swimming plugs, large metal spoons, or parachute jigs close to the bottom of river channels, points and submerged rocks can also be effective during herring season.

Squid are another favorite springtime food of large stripers. When the squid arrive, major rips are generally the best places to find the largest concentrations of big fish. Again, dawn is prime time, especially if you want to watch big stripers wallop a surface plug or squid fly. As the sun rises, causing the bass and bait to move deeper in the rips, break out a wire-line outfit and troll parachute jigs near bottom.

Mackerel and menhaden are two other large baitfish that attract big stripers. Mackerel can be easily caught before a trip in many Northeast locations and are very effective when fished live in deep river holes and around rocky structure washed by ocean swells. Fresh-dead mackerel, either whole or in chunks, can also be fished in these locations with good results.

Schools of menhaden (a.k.a. pogies, bunker) are easy to spot as they flip around on the surface in tightly packed schools. You can either cast-net a big batch of them for your live well or snag single baits with a weighted treble tossed into the school. Simply hook the pogy through its back and allow it to swim near the school. If big bluefish are stealing your baits, try fishing the menhaden on a three-way or fishfinder rig to get it down to stripers cruising below the choppers.

Eels are perhaps the most popular striper bait along the East Coast, and for good reason. Stripers seem to go out of their way to hunt down and slurp up a well-presented "snake." Whether you cast it in the surf, drift or slow-troll it over submerged ledges and boulder fields, or drift it through a rip, a live eel is a killer bait for giant stripers. While live eels can be effective during the day, the best time to fish them is at night, since this is when eels are naturally most active.

In the late fall, watch for migrations of sea herring and shad, which often move in close to shore at this time. This is one of the best times to catch large fish on or near the surface, especially early in the morning. A depthsounder comes in handy when the herring schools move deeper in the water column as the sun rises. When you mark a school on the sounder, try slow-trolling big bunker spoons through the area or drifting a live or fresh-dead herring on the bottom.

Key on Structure

Stripers love structure. If there's a lone rock, wreck or oyster bar along a mile of otherwise barren sand beach, you can bet that stripers will gravitate to it. Reefs, wrecks, boulders, pinnacles, sand shoals, weed beds, ledges, points, bridge pilings, sandbars, holes—any variance in the bottom composition—is likely to hold stripers. In the early season (May and June), lone boulders in just ten feet of water can hold some surprisingly large fish.

As the season progresses, the biggest fish move to deeper structure areas during the day. By midsummer, you may have to search the ledges, shoals, wrecks, pinnacles and rock piles in 60 to 100 feet of water in order to find a good concentration of keepers.

Current Considerations

Like all fish (and some people), striped bass adhere to a simple formula: maximum energy input, minimum energy output. Put another way, this means that stripers, especially resident fish, can usually be found in spots that give them the biggest advantage over their prey. That's why the stripers are frequently found in areas of turbulent water and strong current, such as rips and surf zones, both of which serve to exhaust and disorient baitfish, making them vulnerable to attack.

In your search for a trophy, always seek out areas with strong current. Generally speaking, the stronger the current, the bigger the fish, which is why the mouths of large rivers, open-ocean rips and major inlets give up so many keepers. Big stripers are "lazy" creatures that prefer their food to come to them. They like nothing better than to lurk behind a piece of bottom structure, protected from the current, waiting for a meal to cruise by. This is why they seek out rips, ledges, inlets, points, sandbars and similar structure. Furthermore, the current is often strongest in these spots, which puts the baitfish at a decided disadvantage.

While stripers will often chase bait to the surface in areas with strong current, most of the time you'll find the biggest fish hugging the bottom on the downcurrent side of the structure or along the edge of a rip line. That's why it's often necessary to drift your baits near the bottom or troll with wire line or downriggers. A big fish generally won't move very far to grab something, especially if it looks the least bit suspicious. They are "programmed" to attack bait that is drifting past within a very specific feeding window, depending on the strength of the current. The stronger the current, the smaller the window, and the more closely your lure or bait needs to be presented.

The High Surf

If you're a shorebound fisherman, one of the best places to find big stripers is in the surf. Stripers are built for this type of environment. They patrol the surf line, looking for baitfish or crustaceans caught in the turbulence created by waves crashing against the shore or cresting over a sandbar.

If you like to throw surface plugs, the best time to fish the surf is at first light and dusk, although large stripers will often attack top-water lures during the middle of the day in the early spring and late fall. During the summer months, night fishing produces the most trophies in the surf, especially on live eels and swimming plugs. Soaking dead baits (i.e., squid, mackerel, menhaden, herring and clams) on the bottom of deep holes and troughs often works best during the day, particularly in summer. Remember, use the freshest bait you can find.

From Maine to North Carolina, fall is the best time to take big stripers in the surf as the fish migrate southward along the coast. This is also when pluggers and fly-rodders have their best shot at taking fish on the surface during the daylight hours. From Maine to Cape Cod, surf fishing shines in September. From Cape Cod to Long Island, New York, prime time is usually October and November. From New Jersey to North Carolina, big fish are sometimes caught in the surf well into January.

Work the White Water

In the northern reaches of their range (Cape Cod to Maine), very big stripers can be found patrolling rocky shorelines, islands and exposed ledges fronting the open Atlantic. The key here is to cast your bait, lure or fly as close to the rocks as possible as a swell washes over them, so that your offering is tumbled about in the white water and then sinks below the churning foam to where the fish are cruising. To find the fish, work along a section of shoreline, casting as you go.

At night, anchoring and fishing a dead whole bait, live eel, or chunk on the bottom near these swell-swept areas is also a proven way to take big fish. During the day, slow-trolling a long tube lure along the ledges, over boulder fields and close to the shoreline can be effective.

Big-Fish Techniques

Wire Line

The subject of wire line requires an entire chapter, (see p. 83) if not an entire book. Say what you like about its sporting qualities, but wire-line trolling is simply one of the most effective ways of consistently catching big stripers during the day throughout the season, which is why it's a staple of the charter boat industry. Wire line is effective because it allows a lure to be placed within the feeding window of a striper, which usually means near the bottom. Another major benefit of wire line is that it allows you to cover a large area to locate the fish—such as an entire rip line—without having to set up consecutive drifts, as you would if drifting bait. Trolling wire is not simple, how-ever, and requires a precise knowledge of current speed, boat speed, lure weight and bottom structure, among other things. Make no mistake: the boat operator does the real work.

The most popular lure to fish on wire line is the parachute jig. This simple creation primarily imitates squid but may also resemble many types of large baitfish, such as herring and menhaden. Most anglers rig it with a long strip of pork rind and give the lure a pulsating action by "pumping" the rod.

The bizarre-looking tube-and-worm combo is another great lure for taking big fish. This lure performs best when slow-trolled around large rocks and ledges—the natural habitat of real eels. Red and black tubes generally work best, and most expert "tubers" place a seaworm on the trailing hook for scent and taste appeal. Something to keep in mind: if the tube isn't bumping bottom occasionally, it's not being fished deep enough.

Other wire-line offerings that consistently take big fish include bunker spoons (great around herring and menhaden schools), large swimming plugs and the 9ER umbrella rig, which sports big, soft-plastic swimbaits. Live eels and other natural baits can also be trolled on wire.

Bait Drifting

Drifting natural baits through rip areas on a three-way or fishfinder rig is perhaps even more popular than wire-line trolling when it comes to taking big fish. This technique works best once a concentration of fish has been located, since it limits you to a relatively narrow area compared to trolling. Eels are probably the number-one bait for drift-fishing, but live menhaden, herring, mackerel and scup can be equally effective. Dead, whole baits and chunks work well, too.

The key is to match the weight of your sinker to the current speed. Basically, you want to use the lightest sinker you can get away with and still hold bottom. This makes it easier to feel the subtle pickup of a fish sucking in the bait.

Chunking

Chunking is another highly effective way to attract big stripers in areas with moderate current, such as harbors, coves and large, broad rivers. The trick is to find the right location and tide stage where and when big stripers are known to gather, then anchor up and dole out a sparse line of fresh bait pieces (don't toss out too much or the fish will fill up on the free handouts). Good baits for this exercise include menhaden, herring or mackerel. Once the stripers are drawn to the area by the scent and chunks, hooked baits (and sometimes flies) can be drifted back without weight or hopped over the bottom by adding a rubbercore sinker to the line.

Deep-Jigging

Deep-jigging has long been an effective—and fairly easy—way to take large stripers in deep water (30 to 100 feet). It's especially productive during the midsummer months, when big stripers hold over deep, rip-producing shoals, pinnacles, wrecks and reefs.

The basic strategy is to position the boat ahead of the rip line or piece of bottom structure and free-spool the jig to the bottom. As the boat passes through the rip or over the bottom structure, the jig is "yo-yoed" up and down near bottom or cranked rapidly through the water column. When the drift is finished, the helmsman circles back ahead of the rip and sets up another drift. Note: always be ready for a strike as the jig is free-falling. Large metal diamond jigs are the traditional lures of choice, but fast-sinking bucktails and soft-plastics also work well.

Simple Tips

Buy a Good Depthsounder

Some purists view the use of electronics as cheating, but unless you have a real bead on where a concentration of big bass is holding, you're likely to spend a lot of time trying to locate the action. Also, a depthsounder will allow you to zero in on prime pieces of bottom structure where the bass are holding, such as shoals, ledges, pinnacles, holes, wrecks and individual boulders. Knowing the precise location of fish-holding structure is vital to scoring, especially since the fish often won't move more than a few feet to take your offering.

Once you catch a big fish, make sure you note the exact location of the catch, either on your loran or GPS or by taking land bearings, and record the exact tide stage, weather conditions and water temperature. When the same variables occur another day, chances are good that you'll find more big fish in the same spot. In other words, keep a log.

Research

Here's another simple tip: Spend some time (and money) at your local tackle store. Talk to the employees. Aside from the occasional tight-lipped curmudgeonly types, most tackle-shop employees are a wealth of information. You'd be amazed at how forthcoming some of these people are if you seek their advice. Granted, you can't expect all to be revealed, but at the very least you'll learn where some big fish have been taken recently or what kind of lure is working best. After all, providing bogus information isn't likely to make you a repeat customer. In exchange, share some info on *your* catches and what you've seen out there.

Finally, you can hedge your bets for catching big fish by doing a little research before each trip. Read the weekly fishing periodicals or newspapers or get reports off the Internet. Chat groups have become an extraordinary way to get up-to-the-hour info on where and when big fish are being caught. When you learn about a run of large bass somewhere along the coast, be ready to grab your gear and go. In the search for a trophy striper, you've got to be flexible.

—*Tom Richardson*

TOP SPOTS FOR
A TROPHY

TROPHY FISHING FOR STRIPED BASS

The fact remains that there are certain locales that consistently produce more large fish over the years than other places.

A chapter of this sort is bound to cause no small amount of controversy, especially among those anglers who feel slighted that their favorite striper haunt was left out of the mix. Granted, there are many places other than the ones listed below that give up trophy stripers on a regular basis. In fact, it's possible to hook a 30-pound-plus fish almost *anywhere* in the striper's considerable range, including some surprisingly shallow inshore spots.

However, the fact remains that there are certain locales that have consistently produced more large fish over the years than other places. So, after consulting the record books and seeking the advice of striper gurus along the coast, we've put together the following list of hot spots. Any angler seeking a truly large striped bass would do well to place one or more of them on his itinerary.

1) Chesapeake Bay

As the major spawning ground for East Coast striped bass, Chesapeake Bay sees an influx of "cow" bass in March and April. These female stripers are among the biggest of the population, and all of them must pass through the Chesapeake in order to deposit and fertilize their eggs. While big stripers can be caught throughout the Chesapeake as the fish make their way out of the bay following the spawn, the lion's share of trophies are taken at the famous Chesapeake Bay Bridge-Tunnel. This series of rock islands, bridge pilings and submerged tunnels holds big fish throughout the season, although spring is prime time. Productive techniques include casting topwater plugs next to the rocky islands (best at dawn and dusk), jigging bucktails adorned with soft-plastic tails next to the pilings and over the tunnels, and drifting live and dead baits over the rock-covered tunnels.

Come late fall and early winter (November to January), the mouth of the Chesapeake and the Atlantic shore of Virginia see a return of huge stripers, which are moving through on their southern migration. The fish can be located by watching for birds working over baitfish, but deep-trolling techniques are most productive. Large, deep-diving swimming plugs like the Mann's Stretch 30, heavy bucktail jigs and large metal spoons frequently take the biggest fish at this time. If the weather remains mild, the fast fishing can last well into the new year.

2) Shrewsbury Rocks, New Jersey

This line of submerged rocks off Monmouth Beach is a consistent producer of big stripers throughout the season. One reason Shrewsbury Rocks produces such consistent action is because it's relatively isolated, lying some 15 miles from both Manasquan and Shark Inlets, which tends to limit the number of boats that fish there. The rocky bottom extends from just off the beach out to a mile or so, with the most productive depths being 20 to 30 feet. The big fish arrive in mid-May, with prime early-season action lasting through June. Many anglers score well at this time by fishing live baits or trolling bunker spoons and shad rigs on wire line. The rocks continue to produce plenty of trophies through the summer, a time when chunking and fishing live eels at night works best. Come October, waves of big fish again move through the area, gorging on all kinds of baitfish. November and December are prime months for taking the largest stripers, with good fishing sometimes lasting until Christmas or even New Year's if the weather cooperates.

3) Montauk, New York

Montauk is synonymous with striper fishing, and the surf and rips off this eastern Long Island town produce hundreds of keepers each season. Indeed, it was in this area that a 76-pound striper (the second largest sport-caught striper on record) was taken at night on a live eel by Capt. Bob Rochetta.

Among the surf-fishing fraternity, Montauk is regarded as a mecca. Here, wader-clad anglers hurl plugs, baits and jigs in the shadow of the famous lighthouse, hoping for the strike of a huge fish. Daytime plug-casting is best from late May through June, and again from mid-September through November. The latter period is when you're likely to experience one of the amazing surf blitzes for which Montauk is famous, as large schools of stripers and bluefish move along the shore during their fall migration. During summer, casting live eels and swimming plugs at night is often most effective in the surf.

Boat fishermen score their share of large bass by casting or trolling close to the nearshore rocks, as well as by trolling and chunking in the big rips off the point. In late May, the first waves of big fish move through the area and can often be seen chasing squid on the surface. This is prime time for those who want to catch a keeper on topwater plugs and flies. If nothing is showing on the surface, drifting natural baits or tolling parachute jigs, bunker spoons and tube lures on wire line is a proven way to reach the fish. Wire-line trolling continues to work during the dog days of summer, as does drifting eels and chunk baits through the rips, especially at night. The action picks up again in October and November as droves of stripers move past Montauk on their way south. These are the best months to score a truly large fish, and a time when keepers can again be taken on topwater plugs and big herring flies during daytime surface blitzes. Drifting herring or eels through the rips or trolling flashy bunker spoons and jigs on wire line are two techniques that work well when the fish are holding deep. An important thing to remember about Montauk is that the biggest fish often hang around until Thanksgiving—or even later.

4) Orient Point to Fishers Island, New York

The turbulent waters from Orient Point on eastern Long Island to the western tip of Fishers Island have produced more stripers over 60 pounds than any place on earth. As the tides pour back and forth between Long Island Sound and the open Atlantic, they create huge, bait-holding rips in such well-known spots as The Gut, The Sluiceway, and The Race. Each of these spots is unique in make-up, so you have to learn how to fish them (best tides, best spots, etc.) before keepers start coming over the side.

Fishing here is primarily a boating enterprise, and the season runs from May to December, with November producing some of the biggest fish of the year. Good fishing can even last until December in years of mild weather. Keepers can often be taken on or near the surface in May and early June, when large concentrations of squid migrate through the rips. Trolling parachute jigs on wire line also works well in the early season when the fish move deeper during the mid-day hours. Midsummer sees a change in tactics to drifting live eels and chunk baits through the rips at night, an exercise that demands expert boat-handling skills and an intimate knowledge of the waters. Casting and retrieving eels around the rocks in shallower zones also works well. Another highly effective summer technique for taking big fish during the day involves jigging heavy metal lures (diamond jigs, Kastmasters, etc.) and leadhead jigs just off the bottom in 30 to 100 feet of water.

Come fall, big fish move through the rips on their southward migration, often chasing herring on the surface. Similar to the spring migration, this is a time when keepers can be taken on surface lures and large flies.

5) Watch Hill, Rhode Island

The waters between the eastern tip of Fishers Island and Watch Hill, on the western border of Rhode Island, are rife with boulders and ledges that create big, turbulent rips. The large amount of bait that gets caught in these swift currents attracts lots of big fish throughout the season. Late May is when you'll often find huge bass feeding on squid in the rips, especially in the early morning. At this time, keepers can be taken on large surface plugs worked in the first wave of the rip line, a technique that works best from dawn to about 8:00 in the morning. As the fish

move deeper, trolling parachute jigs on wire line continues to take fish, although snags on rocks and lobster gear can be a problem. Later in the season, many anglers score by trolling big tubes close to the rocks and drifting live eels through the rips. Some huge fish, including two 60-plus-pounders, have also been taken on chunk baits fished on the bottom in recent years.

Surf casters do well by slinging plugs and eels around the rocks in front of the Watch Hill lighthouse and along the adjacent beach. Nighttime is the best time for this pursuit during summer, but late-fall action can last all day. Come October and November, waves of giant stripers move through the rips and along the shore, feeding on herring and other baitfish, often right on the surface. Good fishing can last right up until Thanksgiving. A word of caution: the Watch Hill rips can be very dangerous due to extremely powerful currents and the number of house-sized boulders that rise up to within a few feet of the surface, so an intimate knowledge of the area is required.

6) Block Island, Rhode Island

Like its sister islands of Martha's Vineyard and Nantucket, Block Island hosts a resident population of big stripers throughout the season. The island's shoreline is studded with large rocks that serve as prime targets for plug and fly casters, especially early and late in the season. The North Reef off the northern tip of the island is famous for producing consistent catches of big fish. Pluggers and fly fishermen can work the shallow waters of the reef, while wire-line trollers and eel-drifters do well by fishing the high spots in 40 to 60 feet of water. The latter technique is especially productive at night, but requires a good depth-sounder and precise boat positioning. The rocky southwest corner of Block Island is another great spot for big fish. Trolling a long tube-and-worm combo on wire close to the boulders often works well, as does chunking with menhaden.

Come November, schools of very large fish often migrate past the southern tip of Block Island, feeding on schools of herring in the open ocean. Large flocks of gannets and gulls lead anglers to the action at this time, and it's possible to encounter enormous schools of keeper bass chasing herring on the surface. If the fish are deeper, trolling large bunker spoons and other shiny metal lures around the school works well.

7) Elizabeth Islands, Massachusetts

Once the site of an elite bassing club that existed from the mid- to late 1800s, Cuttyhunk Island and the rest of the Elizabeth Islands chain are legend among striper fishermen. In fact, the rocks off Cuttyhunk produced a 73-pounder that held the world record for nearly 60 years. Early in the season (May and June), keepers can be taken by casting topwater plugs, large herring flies, live herring and live eels close to the rocks along the shore of all the islands. During the summer months, working the nearshore rocks is most productive from first light to around 8:00 a.m., and again at dusk.

The powerful currents that pour through the various "holes" (Robinsons, Quicks, Woods, Canapitsit) between the islands make them ideal spots to find big fish throughout the season, even during the middle of the day. Trolling wire line and drifting live eels and chunk baits are the preferred methods for fishing the holes, since the biggest fish usually hug the bottom. Off the tip of Cuttyhunk, the famous Sow and Pigs Reef is a favorite spot among area charter captains, many of whom score by trolling tube-and-worm combos and swimming plugs close to the rocks. Chunkers also do well on this reef. Anglers need to exercise caution when fishing close to shore along the Elizabeths, as the best spots contain many large, boat-eating rocks. Given that, some good plugging and fly-casting spots include Tarpaulin Cove, French Watering Place, Penikese Island, the southeast tip of Pasque Isand, and Lackey's Bay.

8) Martha's Vineyard & Nantucket, Massachusetts

These two Massachusetts islands are surrounded by a wealth of prime striper habitat, all of which holds big fish from May to November. Mid-May to mid-June is the time to fish both live and dead herring around the rocks along the south and north shores of the Vineyard. Later in the season, trolling long tubes and jigs on wire line or live-lining eels and scup over these same spots become the preferred methods for taking big fish.

The numerous sand shoals surrounding the islands are also famous for producing big bass all season, even during the heat of summer. Off the Vineyard, well-known hot spots include Wasque Rip, Hedge Fence, Middle Ground and Lucas Shoal. Off Nantucket, Rose and Crown, Point Rip, Old Man, Miacomet and Tuckernuck shoals are prime spots to troll deep with wire line or drift eels along the bottom, although the bass may also show on the surface from time to time.

Both the Vineyard and Nantucket offer some of the best surf striper fishing in the world. While it's possible to hang a trophy fish along any part of the shore, the south- and east-facing beaches of both islands attract the most surf casters, primarily because of four-wheel-drive accessibility. Daytime surf action is best early and late in the season, but nighttime is when the majority of big fish are taken. Shore anglers also do well by casting lures and flies around nearshore rocks and at the mouths of salt water ponds, especially on an ebb tide. If you want to get in on the best striper fishing of the entire season, whether you fish from shore or boat, visit the islands from mid-September through early November.

9) Outer Cape Cod, Massachusetts

The continuous stretch of beach running along the eastern edge of Cape Cod from Provincetown to Nauset, is hallowed ground among surf casters. During the '50s, '60s and '70s, a subculture of surfmen roamed these beaches in four-wheel-drive vehicles on a season-long quest for big stripers. While vehicular access is severely limited these days, the Outer Cape continues to produce lots of trophy fish. Peak months for daytime action are May and June, and again in September, October and early November. During July and August, night fishing generally produces the most and biggest fish, especially on live eels and swimming plugs.

Since the Outer Cape is a big place, you really have to put in your time and keep an ear to the ground to learn the whereabouts of recent catches. Famous surf spots to try include The Race near Provincetown, Pochet Hole, Gorilla Hole, Lacounts Hollow, Refrigerator Hole and Nauset Inlet. Boat fishermen also do well here by drifting live eels through deep troughs and over sand bars and grass beds. Trailer-boaters will find launch ramps in Provincetown and Orleans, but caution is advised when entering the open ocean, especially at Nauset Inlet.

10) Kennebec River, Maine

Maine's famous Kennebec River, once the most polluted in the state due to paper and pulpwood operations, has been cleaned up over the years and now produces some excellent striped bass fishing from mid-May through October. School fish, as well as 25-plus-pounders, can be taken along the entire tidal portion from the mouth all the way up to the capital city of Augusta, nearly 40 miles inland. Top spots for the bigger bass include the area around Lee Island just above the town of Phippsburg; the mouth of the Back River and Parker Flats just across from it; Pond Island Shoals at the mouth, and the beaches, islands and rocky coastline that stretch westward to Small Point.

Fly fishermen normally take most of their larger fish during the second half of June, while live-baiters drifting mackerel or eels continue to catch trophies throughout summer and fall. Fresh chunk-baits cast into the white water along rocky shorelines and surf along the lower reaches account for numerous big fish each season, as do trolled swimming plugs and pork-rind-tipped bucktail jigs worked over ledges in 10 to 30 feet of water. Surf casters seeking big bass can fish live eels at night along several miles of beach at the mouth, with access at Popham Beach State Park. Launch ramps are located in most towns along the river including Hallowell, Bath and Phippsburg, and a chart is mandatory for those unfamiliar with the area. Over a dozen guides specializing in stripers operate on the Kennebec and the adjacent Sheepscot River, in which the state record bass of 67 pounds was taken in September of 1977.

Honorable Mentions

Oregon Inlet, North Carolina
Hudson River, New York
Delaware Bay, Delaware
Cape May, New Jersey
Chatham, Massachusetts
Boston Harbor, Massachusetts
Cape Cod Canal, Massachusetts
Merrimack River, Massachusetts
Isles of Shoals, New Hampshire

—Tom Richardson

Conservation for STRIPERS

CONSERVATION FOR STRIPERS

RELEASING YOUR STRIPER

I f you've done any kind of striper fishing, you've probably already had to release a fish or two. Let's face it, in these days of strict bag limits and size restrictions, catch-and-release is a way of life, and will probably stay that way for some time.

In case you're under the impression that released fish don't survive, or that releasing fish can't possibly make a difference in the striper population, think again. Tagging data and laboratory studies prove that catch-and-release does work, and with the number of striper anglers growing by leaps and bounds, there is concern over whether there will be enough fish to go around. Every striper counts, which is why it's so important to be familiar with proper release techniques. Here are some important things to consider on future striper trips.

Fighting Time, Water Temperature & Salinity

Other than injury caused by hooks and mishandling, stress is the major factor affecting post-release survival. Simply put, a fish that is brought to the boat quickly has a much better chance of surviving after release than one that has been exhausted by a lengthy battle. For this reason, many people criticize the use of light tackle, which often results in the fish being fought for long periods of time. An exhausted bass is less likely to resume its normal feeding patterns and is vulnerable to attack from predators. Stress also reduces the fish's ability to fight off diseases and parasites and to heal wounds caused by hooks.

Being cold-blooded, stripers can be greatly affected by changes in water temperature. Consequently, they suffer more stress in water that is above their preferred temperature range. This means that a striper caught in 76-degree water will take longer to recover from a fight or injury than a fish taken in 64-degree water. Water temperature is an important consideration for striper fishermen in the southern portions of the species' range, and for anyone who fishes in shallow water during the summer. In overly warm water, it's best to get the fish to the boat as soon as possible and release it quickly.

Salinity also affects the recovery time of stripers. Studies have shown that fish caught in areas of low salinity, such as the upper portions of estuaries, are less likely to survive after release than bass taken in pure ocean water. Again, if you fish in low-salinity areas, it's

Every striper counts, which is why it's so important to be familiar with proper release techniques.

best to get the fish in quickly and release it immediately.

Limit Handling Time

As a general rule, always try to limit the amount of time you keep a fish out of the water. In fact, the best possible scenario is to keep the fish in the water while you remove the hook. Swinging the fish onboard and allowing it to flop around on deck is obviously not ideal, since this can cause internal injuries and further exhaustion. When removing the hook, hold the striper firmly by its lower jaw and avoid touching its body with your hands, clothing or other objects, which can remove the protective coating of slime that protects the fish from infection, parasites and disease.

If you must bring the fish onboard, either grasp it by the lower lip or use a landing device such as the Boga Grip. If you prefer to use a net, select one with a shallow rubber or cotton mesh basket that doesn't bend the fish too severely or remove lots of slime and scales. A good technique with large stripers is to place them on a soft, wet surface, such as a wet towel or piece of foam laid on the deck. Covering the fish's head and body with a towel will also calm it and keep the skin moist. If your boat has a salt water washdown, keep a gentle stream of water flowing over the fish's gills and body.

Perhaps the most important thing you can do is remove the hook and get the fish back in the water as soon as possible. The longer the fish is kept out of the water, the lower its chances of post-release survival, particularly if it has endured a lengthy fight.

Many fish will simply swim off energetically after being returned to the water, particularly if they were brought to the boat quickly and in good shape. However, others may require a little extra help, so don't just toss the fish back in the water and walk away. To revive an exhausted fish, grasp its jaw between your thumb and forefinger and gently move it back and forth in the water to get oxygen flowing over its gills. Some fish may take a long time to recover, but stay with it. When the striper clamps down on your thumb, it's generally a good sign that the fish is ready to swim off on its own.

Watch Those Hooks!

Where a fish is hooked can definitely make a big difference in its ability to survive release. For example, a jaw-hooked fish stands a much better chance of survival than a fish that's hooked in the gills or stomach. This is why many bait fishermen have switched to circle hooks in recent years. A circle hook can actually be swallowed by the fish but will slide out of the stomach when it moves off with the bait. As the line is pulled through the fish's mouth, it guides the hook around the jaw, where it "locks" in place upon encountering resistance. Many striper fishermen report no reduction in the amount of hook-ups they get with circle hooks, and some even say the hooks have increased their catch.

Large plugs rigged with multiple treble hooks can cause a lot of injury to a striper, since the free hooks often swing around and catch in the fish's gills or eye. Also, removing the multiple barbs can increase the amount of time the fish is kept out of the water. To reduce the risk of injury, simply remove the extraneous trebles or snip off the barbs with a pair of pliers. At the very least, crush the barbs on the trebles to make the hooks easier to remove. You can also rig some plugs with barbless single hooks without affecting their action.

A gill- or stomach-hooked fish presents a problem. With the former, you must be very careful to remove the hooks, as the gills are extremely delicate and vital organs. Above all, never try to rip the hooks out of the fish's mouth in desperation. Instead, cut the line and carefully pull the hook or lure through the gills with long-nosed pliers. With a fish that's hooked in the stomach or deep in the throat, use a long-handled tool (see opposite page) that allows you to push the hook backwards in order to dislodge it.

If there's no way to remove the hook, the only answer is to cut the line as close to the hook eye as possible and hope for the best. Although hooks should always be removed whenever possible, stripers can and do survive with hooks still embedded in their flesh, especially if the fish are healthy and environmental conditions are ideal.

Tools of the Trade

There are numerous release tools on the market, ranging from homemade jobs to expensive stainless steel devices. For starters, a good pair of long-nosed pliers can be a big help in removing hooks caught in the jaw, throat or gills. A simple J-shaped hook remover, which can be fashioned from an old paint roller, allows you to remove the hook (if lodged in the jaw) without touching the fish at all. To use, slip the bend of the "J" around the hook bend, then lift while pulling down on the leader with your other hand. The weight of the fish and a little jiggling will often cause it to fall off the hook, especially if you go barbless.

There are several types of long-handled tools for dislodging hooks that are caught in a striper's stomach or throat. To use, slide the end of the tool along the leader until it reaches the bend in the hook, clamp down on the line with your thumb to keep it taut, and push the hook backwards.

The Baker Hook-Out and the Fish-Hook Extractor are two excellent tools for removing hard-to-reach hooks. Both allow you to grip the hook shank firmly so you can work it free. A nifty device for controlling fish at boatside is the Boga Grip. It's expensive (around $100), but its pincers maintain a secure yet non-damaging grip on the fish while you go about the work of removing the hook. It also features a scale in the handle for weighing your catch. If you don't want to shell out big bucks for a Boga Grip, there are inexpensive, plastic fish-grippers on the market that do an equally good job of holding the fish's jaw.

—*Tom Richardson*

DEVICES FOR HANDLING THE FISH AND REMOVING HOOKS will decrease the amount of time it takes to unhook and release a fish, improving its chances for survival.

CONSERVATION FOR STRIPERS

MANAGING STRIPED BASS: WHERE DO WE GO FROM HERE?

S triped bass are as American as apple pie, bourbon whiskey and pickup trucks. Maybe more so! From the early references of Pilgrim John Smith, who wrote that one could walk "dri-shod" across the backs of the bass, to modern times when descendants of the Santee-Cooper impoundment striped bass stocks inhabit fresh water lakes in almost every state in the Lower 48, this fish has been held in near mystical reverence. The elusive nature of the larger adult fish and the desirability of its meat as table fare have made the striped bass a target of too many people.

In colonial days, striped bass were incredibly abundant and fishing pressure was minimal. The same can be said of Atlantic salmon, which are now largely gone from the New England rivers where they once spawned populations in the hundreds of thousands. In those early days, the Pilgrims could walk the beaches of Plymouth and Kingston Bays at low tide and pluck lobsters from the tidal pools. Of course, this is no longer possible. We humans have left our indelible fingerprint on most of our marine resources and their habitats.

From the colonial days of incredible abundance, the population of striped bass has fluctuated naturally in size; however, fishing pressure and habitat degradation have exacerbated these natural highs and lows. In the late 1970s, many fishermen and scientists thought that a total collapse of the Chesapeake Bay striped bass stock was at hand. Today, the stocks of all Atlantic Coast striped bass are much healthier, due in part to very restrictive management regimes and the good graces of Mother Nature, who provided several outstanding spawning years. It should also be noted that many of those states that were unwilling participants in the management plan now step to the head of the line when praise is being handed out for saving the stripers. There is concern, however, that the light at the end of the tunnel may be another oncoming problem. It may be time to reassess current management strategies.

Stocks of striped bass along the East Coast appear to be flourishing, but management and allocation questions loom on the horizon.

The Case for Game Fish Status

With spawning stocks in the Chesapeake declared fully restored, many fishery managers and commercial interests insist that there is no "conservation" basis for officially designating striped bass a game fish, which would outlaw the sale of wild stripers and eliminate the commercial fishery for them. There is some, but not substantial, disagreement with this position. What is obvious, though, are the overwhelming economic reasons for using all striped bass to generate their highest value and to spread this value over the greatest number of users. There is also a strong case to be made that the true commercial user of the striper resource is, in fact, the recreational industry.

There are several indisputable facts that are important parts of the equation. (1) Striped bass carry a higher economic value as a recreationally harvested fish than they do as a commercially harvested fish. (2) Nearshore recreational fishermen along the Atlantic Coast have very few alternative species to fish for since most others have been commercially overharvested. (3) Recreational fishermen supply many times more meals for public consumption than the commercial industry does. (4) The resource can theoretically be overharvested by the recreational fishery alone, leaving no excess amount of stripers to be harvested commercially. Looking at each one of these points may help to bring about a better understanding of the fishery and a possible solution to the dilemma facing fishery managers.

Simple Economics

First, let's examine the issue of economic value. The figures used in the following comparisons were not pulled out of thin air. They are numbers generated in 1995 by Southwick Associates (an economic consulting firm) for the Atlantic States Marine Fisheries Commission (ASMFC) to quantify the economic impact of the striped bass fishery from Maine to North Carolina during 1993. Direct sport-fishing expenditures on striped bass trips increased from $85 million in 1981 to $560 million in 1996, which represents an

annual growth of 35%. Overall, the total economic impact of recreationally caught striped bass in 1993 was many times greater than that generated by the commercial sector—$252,642,274 recreational to $53,611,000 commercial. It should be noted that the study indicated that simply adding up the economic impact of each state would understate the total impact, as those numbers did not include interstate trade. The state numbers have been added but it is felt that since they applied to both sectors equally, their relation to the final result would remain the same. The study did a state-by-state analysis for the recreational industry, while the commercial industry was broken down by region.

On a per-pound basis for all states from Maine to North Carolina, recreationally caught fish were worth $40 each and commercially caught fish were worth $31. On a regional basis, this value varied substantially. In New England, the ratio was almost four to one in favor of the recreational side, with $81 per pound versus $21. In the Mid-Atlantic region it was just about even, and in the South Atlantic it was two-to-one recreational. According to figures from the National Marines Fisheries Service (NMFS) Marine Recreational Fishing Survey, fishing trips from Maine through North Carolina that targeted striped bass exceeded eight million in 1997, up from 1 million in 1981, and approximately one out of every four fishing trips in 1996 and 1997 targeted striped bass.

The recreational striped bass fishery directly employs 2.6 times more people than the commercial sector. Sport fishing for stripers generates over $11 million in state taxes and more than five times the federal taxes generated by the commercial industry. So from an economic standpoint, it does not take a lot of figuring to conclude that striped bass caught by recreational fishermen are a better use of a limited resource. Any fish taken by the commercial sector has the potential of reducing the full economic activity that could be produced by that fish.

How Many Anglers?

The key words here are "limited resource." Although different managers have varying opinions as to who should get what and what the size of the biomass means, few would dispute that with today's technology, humans have the potential to overfish the resource, whether it's done with nets or rods.

If something were to happen to striped bass (which the ASMFC says "cannot"), what are the alternatives for the nearshore recreational fisherman along the Atlantic coast? Some would say that recreational fishermen do not need a lot of fish to catch. They say that "recs" just like to go out, dangle their worm over the side and drink beer. If that were true, how does one explain the substantial increase in interest, activity and sales stimulated by the recent growth of the striped bass population?

Unfortunately, since NMFS has never made a coordinated effort to generate recreational fishing statistics on the level they have for commercial harvesters, the number of recreational participants in the striped bass fishery over the past 20 years is somewhat elusive. However, more recent catch statistics are known. According to NMFS, recreational anglers caught more striped bass in the last two years (1994-95) than the total amount caught from 1984 to 1993, and that number continues to grow. The 1995 – 1997 average total striped bass catch is almost 2.5 times the 1992 – 1994 average striped bass catch. The total estimated weight of recreationally harvested striped bass in 1997 (14.86 million pounds) exceeded the 1996 estimate and was the highest recorded since the Marine Recreational Fisheries Statistical Survey began. This total at least proves that recreational fishermen are interested in actually catching fish. At the same time, however, anglers are concerned that ASMFC does not have a good handle on what the growth curve in participation has been historically, and therefore does not have a good ability to predict the future. Even though ASMFC does not have good participation numbers, it continually raises the red flag over increased recreational participation.

What Else to Fish For?

The vast majority of species that have traditionally been targeted by recreational fishermen are listed as overexploited by the NMFS in its annual *Status of the Fishery Resources* publication. Such Mid-Atlantic staples as weakfish, fluke, and bluefish are in short supply. In the Northeast, tautog, black sea bass, scup, winter flounder and bluefish are all overexploited. Since recreational fishermen have few inshore species to fish for, many have turned their attention to stripers. Also, many anglers catch striped bass incidentally while fishing for other species. These factors make it difficult for ASMFC to estimate the growth in the recreational effort in the striped bass fishery. The bottom line is that the recreational industry will suffer the biggest loss if striped bass go into another decline.

One of the prime arguments for conducting a commercial bass fishery is that commercial harvesters supply the public with fish. But so do sport fishermen. In 1995, the recreational industry harvested 12.1 million pounds of striped bass and the commercial sector just 3.8 million pounds. That means recreational fishermen put over three times the number of striped bass meals on the table than commercial fishermen did. Therefore, it is recreational fishermen who do a more efficient job of getting fish protein into the mouths of the fish-consuming public.

If U.S. fisheries managers used the New Zealand model for allocation of marine resources, they would allow recreational fishermen to take their share and give the remainder to the commercial side. However, even if this was the case, a close look at the numbers indicates that there might not be any stripers left to allocate after the recreational side is allocated its share. In fact, there is a lot of evidence that anglers may already be exceeding the desired harvest levels.

Recreational Overfishing Possible

According to ASMFC's 1996 estimated Atlantic striped bass harvest figures, commercial fishermen took 5.4 million pounds of fish, while recreational fishermen took 12.4 million. Amendment Five to the Striped Bass Management Plan has an annual target mortality for 1998 and 1999 of F = .31. "F" stands for total mortality in the formula used to calculate the desired harvest levels, but it is not the actual percentage of the population. Total

mortality includes all fish that are kept by fishermen, those that die after being released, those that die naturally and those that are discarded dead as bycatch in other fisheries. The figures for 1997 calculated by some of the scientists working on the ASMFC plan indicate that the 1997 mortality for striped bass was close to the target of .31. By itself, this would not indicate a serious problem. However, fishermen have the potential to easily reach and exceed that level. Projections for 1999 show the harvest increasing to 6.4 million commercial pounds and 16.3 million recreational pounds.

At the July 1996 meeting of the ASMFC, the Striped Bass Technical Committee expressed some concern over the mortality figures it was seeing. This committee told the Striped Bass Management Board of its concern and indicated several possible ways of addressing it. The management board, realizing that it was playing with a very hot political potato, made no decision and called for another meeting. This delay allowed time to complete an ongoing virtual population analysis for striped bass, which should give statistically valid mortality figures. However, many believe that this inability to reach a management decision was compounded by the existence of a commercial fishery for striped bass. It may also be an indicator of troubled management decisions to come.

It should also be noted that managers routinely tell recreational participants that the huge numbers of 20- to 22-inch fish will soon turn into large numbers of big fish. However, every year the population dynamics of striped bass seem to remain skewed to the smaller fish. For the average sport fisherman the size distribution seems to change very little.

The harvesting of millions of pounds of 18-inch fish in the Chesapeake Bay area and a coastal regime of harvesting over-28-inch fish may well be major factors in the population dynamics. New management alternatives will have to be considered.

Participation Growing

Most, if not all, of the increased mortality is caused by growing participation in the recreational fishery. This is obviously due to the increased popularity of striped bass and the lack of viable alternative species available to recreational fishermen in many coastal areas.

There are other troubling statistics that do not seem to get much press. Indicative of the demand being put on striped bass, NMFS numbers show that the 1994-95 total average catch (including those fish released alive) of 9.6 million stripers was more than twice the total average catch for 1992-93. Can that trend continue without serious plan modifications?

Concern is also growing over the length-to-weight ratios of striped bass. The average weight for certain lengths is declining. This indicates a problem with the forage base and also the necessity of total ecosystem management. Fisheries managers cannot allow continued overharvest of menhaden, squid and other food fish important to striped bass.

One theory about the weight problem, unproven at this time, says that striped bass released by recreational anglers do not feed for a period of time and therefore suffer weight reduction. Due to the decreased forage base in many areas, it is theorized that they are unable to make up the loss. This is a real reach, but it has the potential to impact recreational anglers.

Also, if one takes a look at the approximate number of participants in the recreational striped bass fishery, more potential problems seem to surface. It should be noted that NMFS and ASMFC do not have any valid estimates on the number of participants in the striped bass fishery, yet both groups say the striped bass fishery is the most studied and controlled

fishery in the U.S. marine environment. By looking at the average number of trips taken by all fishermen and comparing it to the number of trips taken by striped bass fishermen, a figure of approximately 1.5 million participants for 1995 emerges. Then look at the same numbers for the state of Maryland, which issues striped bass stamps and therefore has a good handle on the number of participants. Again the figure is very close to 1.5 million. A third method of determining the number of recreational striper fishermen used the ratio of striped bass fishing trips to all fishing trips to reach another figure, which, although smaller, approximated the 1.5 million estimate. Using the same methods, the approximate number of participants grew to 2 million in 1997. Because of the increasing popularity of the striper and the strong growth in angling participation, the approximate participation numbers should be considered very conservative.

The 1995 recreational harvest of stripers was 1.1 million fish. If each participant caught and kept only one daily limit of striped bass per year, the 1995 recreational harvest numbers would have almost doubled. This ratio also applies for 1997. Although fishery managers would say that the restrictions in place would make such a harvest virtually impossible, these numbers do show that there is a very limited striper resource. It would also be interesting to know if the average number of trips per angler was increasing or if the overall participation was increasing, or both.

Management Alternatives

Should managers look at other management tools that aren't currently being used in the striped bass fishery? Should there be a total paradigm shift in management philosophy? Why not make striped bass a game fish and allocate the entire resource to the general public? There are too many arguments in favor of this option to have it so thoroughly discarded as a management tool.

Since fishery managers, by their very nature, are reluctant to get involved in allocation issues, there is often a sense that legislative solutions will have to prevail. However, it is evident that if game fish status were given to striped bass in every state, the steps necessary to ensure healthy stocks for the long haul could be more easily put in place. Giving the total allocation to the recreational users would not eliminate the necessity for strict management controls.

From an economic standpoint, game fish status is the logical course. From a social standpoint, the greatest numbers of users are in the recreational sector, whereas the number of commercial fishermen is minimal. For example, in Massachusetts in 1995, there were approximately 465,000 recreational striped bass fishermen and 3,353 commercial permits, of which only 982 were active (an "active" permit holder is someone who has a record of commercial sale). For the same year in Maryland, there were 221,000 recreational striper fishermen and 1,231 commercial striped bass permits. Does the current management strategy make sense when a few can take thousands of fish and profit from them, while the vast majority may not even be able to catch a single day's limit?

So what about the commercial sale of striped bass in markets and restaurants? Will the general public no longer be able to enjoy striped bass? Although there is some question from a taste standpoint about the current farm-raised bass, the technology is available to produce a product that is identical to the wild fish—at less cost to the consumer.

Release Survival

There has been a lot of concern over release mortality in the recreational fishery and in those states where the commercial harvest is by hook and line. ASMFC has used a figure of 8 percent release mortality in both fisheries. This may well have to be modified by area and date of catch. For instance, studies have shown that fish hooked in the stomach or throat have a higher mortality. Since using bait, live or dead, is such an effective method of taking stripers and is the predominant method in the commercial fishery, particularly in the Northeast, the release mortality in that category should be reanalyzed. Also, no matter who hooks and releases the fish, water temperature is the most critical factor. Above a certain temperature, there is almost a

100 percent mortality of released fish, so managers should look into time and area closures in certain estuaries during appropriate periods of the year. Whatever happens with allocation issues, ASMFC needs to work diligently to decrease release mortality.

Even though release mortality may be high in the recreational sector, it needs to be put in perspective. In Massachusetts, for example, there were approximately 465,000 recreational striped bass anglers in 1995. The release mortality in their fishery caused an estimated 262,000 striped bass to die inadvertently. That amounts to approximately ½ fish per angler per season. The number of active striped bass commercial permit holders in Massachusetts for 1995 was 982, and the number of released fish that died in that fishery was estimated at 17,300. That amounts to approximately 17.5 fish per commercial harvester per season. This begs the question as to where the real problem may lie.

What About Slot Limits?

The current management scheme uses minimum size limits as one of its main tools. There is not a problem with this, but the addition of maximum size limits would also be beneficial. This management measure is called a slot limit. There are several benefits to using a slot limit. With the existing size limits and increasing fishing participation, most legal-size bass will be cropped off annually. The current minimum size limits will always eliminate the bulk of the large breeding females, which as 25- to 40-pound fish are far more fecund and produce many more eggs than fish under the 25-pound mark.

From a biological standpoint, the large fish are predominantly females. Leaving the smaller males while cropping off the larger females may well cause an imbalance in the spawning biomass. In the long run, a slot limit will create a better distribution of fish sizes and will make for a far better fishery, both biologically and qualitatively. Recreational fishermen want the chance to make that once-in-a-lifetime catch, and a wider distribution of fish sizes increases that potential. From the recreational standpoint, just having a lot of small fish to catch does not constitute a quality fishery.

As for keeping that larger fish, some mechanism could be set up to allow the taking of an occasional "trophy."

A slot limit would also minimize the tendency for fishermen to practice what is known as high-grading. This simply means that if the minimum size is 28 inches and the fisherman has already filled his one- or two-fish limit, he might be tempted to discard the smallest fish if he catches a bigger one. A slot limit with a narrow window of, say, 24 to 30 inches would minimize this temptation.

It is also evident that with the growing interest in striped bass fishing, there will likely have to be some additional restrictions placed on recreational fishermen, even if stripers are made a game fish. Establishing fishing seasons is certainly one possibility. ASMFC will have to gather more detailed information on the numbers and trends of recreational participants. They will also have to investigate uniform management schemes that treat all areas of the coast equally in terms of size limits, catch limits, and quotas, something that's not happening today.

If striped bass is the management success story that most fishery managers say it is while liberally patting themselves on the back, then it may well be the only major success interjurisdictional fisheries management has had. It could be described as the only jewel in ASMFC's tarnished management crown. As such, many of us wonder why managers would not be cherishing this jewel and managing it as conservatively as possible. Maybe some people think that they are.

The future of striped bass is not a clear picture, and management goals are likely to be moving targets. There are many factors that affect this fish, not the least of which is its relatively fragile spawning habitat. It is our obligation as anglers to keep an eye on and protect all of our marine ecosystems if there are to be any fisheries available to us in the future. It is also our obligation to let fishery managers know what the public wants and not allow them to operate in an ivory tower of scientific knowledge and isolation. Fishery managers have done a good job of restoring striped bass for the last years of the 20th century, but it is up to the users of this resource to work with them to create a plan that will maintain a healthy resource and maximize its benefits well into the 21st century.

—*Rip Cunningham*

Index

Creative Publishing international, Inc.
offers a variety of how-to books.
For information write:
    Creative Publishing international, Inc.
    Subscriber Books
    5900 Green Oak Drive
    Minnetonka, MN 55343

143

Author Biographies

Tim Coleman has fished from different beaches and rock piles since he was six. He's based a lot of life's decisions on his need to be near the water. His interest in angling was interrupted by Vietnam, and afterwards, a B.A. degree in journalism from the University of Rhode Island. For the last 25 years he's been the Managing Editor of *The New England Fisherman* and the Senior Editor of *The Fisherman Group*. During that time he's written over 1,000 articles, columns and editorials.

✦

Rip Cunningham, an avowed striper addict, can cast a fly line or muscle a billfish with the pros, but he is best known amongst the sport fishing fraternity for his hard-hitting, conservation-oriented editorials in *Salt Water Sportsman* magazine. As Editor-in-Chief and Publisher of America's #1 sport fishing magazine, Rip continues *Salt Water Sportsman's* 60-year tradition of promoting sensible marine resource management. He has also been very active in fisheries management at the state and federal levels.

✦

Barry Gibson is the longtime Editor of *Salt Water Sportsman* magazine and has been fishing for striped bass — his favorite species — for over 40 years. A charter boat captain in Boothbay Harbor, Maine, since 1971, he currently runs a 24-foot center-console and guides exclusively for stripers in the Kennebec and Sheepscot river systems. His personal-best bass to date is a 53-pounder taken at night from the surf on a Maine beach in September of 1980.

✦

Nick Karas has been the outdoors columnist for *New York Newsday* for the last 25 years and is a frequent contributor to numerous other publications, including *Salt Water Sportsman, South Coast Sportfishing* and the *New York Times*. Nick has more than a dozen books to his credit. His classic tome, *The Striped Bass,* is in its second edition. His *Guide to Salt Water Fishing,* an annual publication since 1985, serves salt water anglers who fish in New York Bight waters.

Tom Richardson is Managing Editor of *Salt Water Sportsman* magazine, as well as a contributing writer to the on-line fishing magazine *Reel-Time*. He has fished for striped bass from the Chesapeake to Maine, but spends most of his time on the waters of southern Massachusetts, Cape Cod and Rhode Island.

✦

Allan J. (Al) Ristori has been fishing for over a half-century. Al has written thousands of magazine articles and has long served as a regional editor for *Salt Water Sportsman*, where his first national article was published in 1965. Al is also the author of *North American Saltwater Fishing, The Saltwater Fish Identifier* and *Fishing for Bluefish*. He's fished over much of the world, holds several world records and is a Coast Guard licensed charter boat captain.

✦

Vin T. Sparano has been an outdoor editor and writer for more than 35 years. Currently, Vin is Editor Emeritus/Senior Field Editor of *Outdoor Life*, having served as Editor in Chief from 1990-1995 and previously as Executive Editor for more than 10 years. He has authored 18 books and a vast number of articles for national magazines and newpapers. He has fished and hunted the world and continues to share his outdoor experiences and knowledge through his writings and speaking engagements. Vin lives in Barnegat Light on Long Beach Island, NJ, where he is a familiar sight fishing from his boat, the *Betty Boop*.

✦

Lou Tabory has been an outdoor writer for over 30 years, with articles in many major sporting publications, including *Field & Stream, Outdoor Life, Sports Afield, Salt Water Sportsman, Fly Fisherman, Salt Water Fly Fishing, Fly Fishing in Salt Water* and *American Angler*. Lou has also authored the books *Inshore Fly Fishing* and *Lou Tabory's Guide to Saltwater Baits and Their Imitations*. He has salt water fly fished for over three decades and is considered one of the early pioneers in the Northeast, having invented a number of flies for marine fishing.

Photo & Illustration Credits